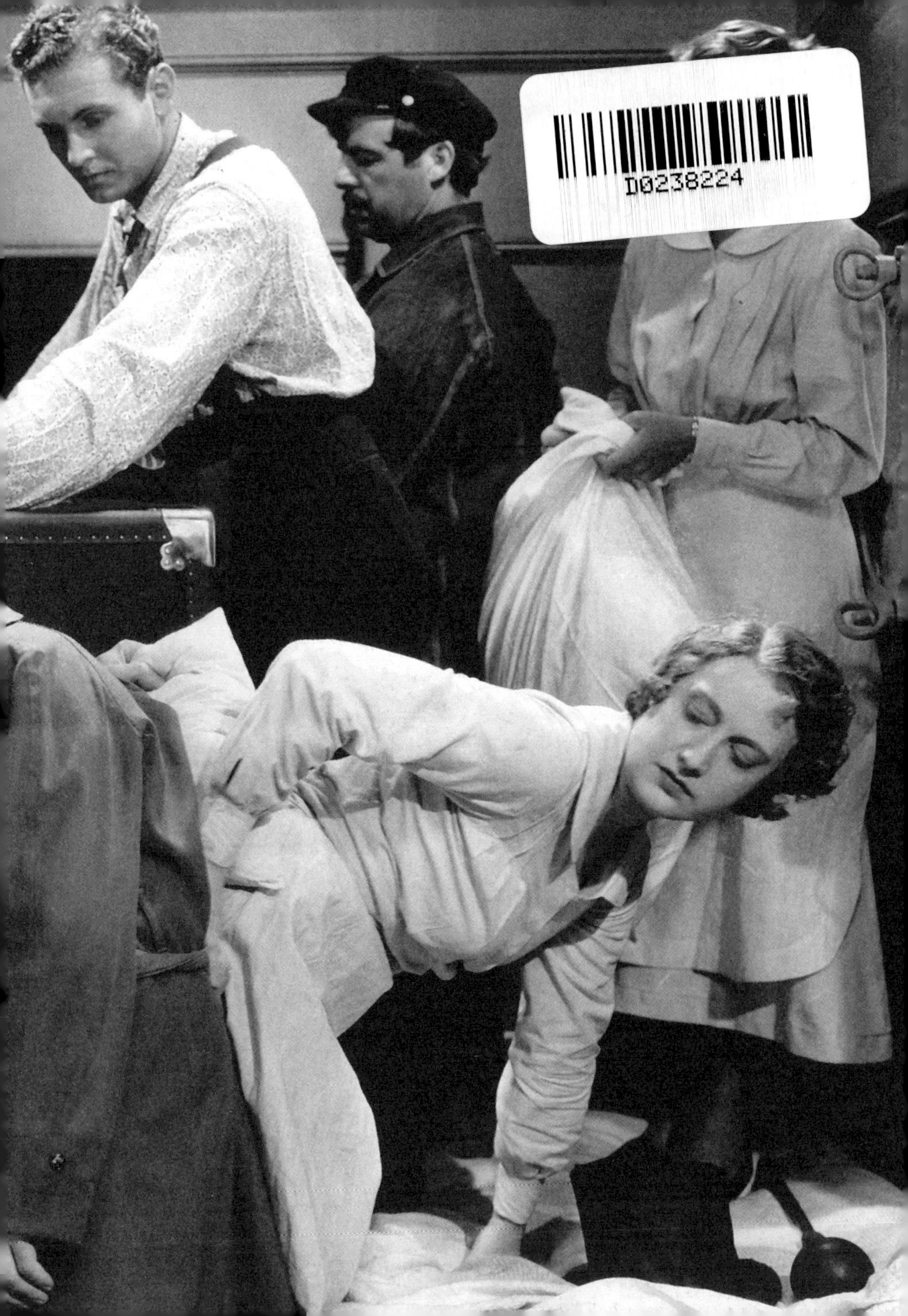

MOVIE ★ ICONS

MARX BROS.

EDITOR
PAUL DUNCAN

TEXT
DOUGLAS KEESEY

PHOTOS
THE KOBAL COLLECTION

TASCHEN
HONG KONG KÖLN LONDON LOS ANGELES MADRID PARIS TOKYO

CONTENTS

1

THE MARX BROTHERS: INSANELY FUNNY

BY DOUGLAS KEESEY

DIE MARX BROTHERS: IRRE WITZIG

LES MARX BROTHERS : LES FOUS DU RIRE

THE MARX BROTHERS: INSANELY FUNNY

by Douglas Keesey

The Marx Brothers – Groucho, Chico, Harpo and sometimes Zeppo – spent over 20 years perfecting their comic timing in vaudeville routines and Broadway theatre revues before becoming one of cinema's most successful comedy teams. They made 13 films together between 1929 and 1949, including *Duck Soup* (1933), *A Night at the Opera* (1935), and *A Day at the Races* (1937), and appeared separately in dozens of additional film and television roles.

Groucho is immediately recognizable with his big cigar, bushy eyebrows, greasepaint moustache and stooped walk. He would impersonate authority figures in a way that lampooned their pomposity, whether as Captain Jeffrey T. Spaulding, Dr. Hugo Z. Hackenbush or Attorney J. Cheever Loophole. Brother Zeppo played the straight man to wisecracking Groucho, taking a relentless ribbing. Groucho once said, "The only surefire way to test out a new gag was to try it out on Zeppo. If he liked it, we threw it out." Despite the fact that Zeppo, with his handsome profile and manly tenor voice, also got to play the romantic lead, he eventually left the act after five films, saying "I'm sick and tired of being the stooge." His newspaper obituary later described him as 'the Marx Brother who got the girl but never the gags.' Another famous foil for Groucho's humor was Margaret Dumont, who for seven films played a high-society lady subjected to Groucho's insults and innuendoes: "There are many bonds that will hold us together throughout eternity – your government bonds, your savings bonds, your Liberty bonds." "Would you mind giving me a lock of your hair? I'm letting you off easy. I was going to ask for the whole wig." Groucho always insisted that what made Dumont such a perfect straight woman was her bewilderment – she never understood his jokes. He praised her highly in calling her "practically the fifth Marx Brother."

Chico (pronounced 'chick-o') was characterized by his leprechaun hat, rakish grin and patently fake Italian accent. On screen and off, Chico was a lovable con artist, a compulsive

GROUCHO MARX

"Quote me as saying I was misquoted."
Groucho

gambler and womanizer (chasing the 'chicks'). According to Groucho, "There were three things that Chico was always on – a phone, a horse or a broad." In the movies, Chico pitted his street smarts against brainy authority figures, outsmarting Groucho at the racetrack by selling him one betting guide after another, each more worthless than the last. Chico also threatened to outwit Groucho at a land auction, mischievously punning on "viaduct": "Why a duck? Why-a no chicken?" Through Chico the lowly but triumphant schemer, 'immigrants could take a liberating revenge on that American xenophobia that made them feel like third-class citizens,' as Raymond Durgnat wrote. Even Chico's way of playing the piano was clever, for he would extend his right forefinger to 'shoot' the keys.

Harpo played the harp like an angel, causing listeners to cry, but he behaved like a little devil, often bringing tears of frustration to the eyes of those he taunted. Under a woolly wig and battered top hat, Harpo's cherubic face could turn gargoyle when he puffed out his cheeks and crossed his eyes to make his patented 'gookie' face. In one film, a hotel detective can only watch, stupefied, as a cascade of stolen silverware falls out of Harpo's coat sleeves, culminating with a coffeepot. In another movie, thugs search Harpo's coat pockets for stolen jewels, but find instead a welcome mat, a barber's pole, a sled, a block of ice, and a live dog. (But when a man in need asks for some change, Harpo can pull from his coat a steaming hot cup of coffee.) In some ways, Harpo was like a naughty child forever defiant of father figures, as when he would go around cutting off men's cigars, neckties and coattails. Bill Marx, Harpo's son, once said: "My Dad never went through his second childhood, because he never got out of his first." In other ways, Harpo was like an ever-priapic Pan, placing his leg in the hands of ladies like Margaret Dumont or running after blondes while honking his horn.

There is obviously much method to the Marx Brothers' madness, but is there a message? Perhaps Harpo said it best: "If things get too much for you and you feel the whole world's against you, go stand on your head. If you can think of anything crazier to do, do it."

ENDPAPERS/VOR- UND NACHSATZBLÄTTER/
PAGES DE GARDE
STILLS FROM 'A NIGHT AT THE OPERA' (1935)

PAGES 2/3
THE THREE MARX BROTHERS (1935)

PAGE 4
THE THREE MARX BROTHERS (1935)

PAGES 6/7
PORTRAIT FOR 'A DAY AT THE RACES' (1937)

PAGE 8
THE THREE MARX BROTHERS

OPPOSITE/RECHTS/CI-CONTRE
GROUCHO MARX

THE MARX BROTHERS: IRRE WITZIG

von Douglas Keesey

Bevor sie zu einem der erfolgreichsten Comedy-Teams der Filmgeschichte wurden, perfektionierten die Marx Brothers – Groucho, Chico, Harpo und manchmal Zeppo – ihre Komik und ihr Timing zwei Jahrzehnte lang auf den Bühnen des Varietétheaters und der Broadwayrevuen. Zwischen 1929 und 1949 drehten sie gemeinsam 13 Filme, darunter *Die Marx Brothers im Krieg* (1933), *Die Marx Brothers in der Oper* (aka *Skandal in der Oper*, 1935) und *Ein Tag beim Rennen* (aka *Das große Rennen/Auf der Rennbahn*, 1937). Daneben traten sie getrennt in Dutzenden weiterer Filme und Fernsehprogramme auf.

Groucho erkennt man auf einen Blick an seiner dicken Zigarre, seinen buschigen Augenbrauen, seinem dick aufgemalten Schnauzer und eigentümlichen Gang. Er spielte Autoritätspersonen so, dass ihr aufgeblasenes Gehabe lächerlich wirkte, sei es Captain Jeffrey T. Spaulding, Dr. Hugo Z. Hackenbush oder der Rechtsanwalt J. Cheever Loophole. Sein Bruder Zeppo mimte für den kalauernden Groucho den ehrbaren Kerl, der stets dessen erbarmungslose Frotzeleien über sich ergehen lassen musste. Groucho sagte einmal: „Die einzig hundertprozentig sichere Methode, einen neuen Gag zu testen, war, ihn an Zeppo auszuprobieren. Wenn er ihm gefiel, dann schmissen wir den Gag raus." Obwohl Zeppo mit seinen gefälligen Zügen und seiner maskulinen Tenorstimme die Liebhaberrollen übernehmen durfte, verließ er die Gruppe nach fünf Filmen, weil er es leid war, immer nur den Handlanger zu spielen. In einem Nachruf auf ihn schrieb eine Zeitung später, er sei der Marx Brother gewesen, der „die Frauen, aber nie die Gags" bekommen habe. Ein weiteres berühmtes Opfer von Grouchos Humor war Margaret Dumont, die in sieben Filmen die feine Dame verkörperte, die von Groucho mit Beleidigungen und anzüglichen Bemerkungen überhäuft wurde: „Es gibt so viele ‚bonds' (Bande), die uns auf ewig aneinanderbinden werden – Ihre ‚government bonds' (Schatzbriefe), Ihre ‚savings bonds' (Sparbriefe) und Ihre ‚liberty bonds' (Kriegsanleihen)." – „Würde es Ihnen etwas ausmachen, mir eine Locke Ihres Haares zu geben? Ich mach's Ihnen leicht. Eigentlich wollte ich nämlich die ganze Perücke." Groucho behauptete immer, Dumont sei deshalb eine so hervorragende Zielscheibe für seinen Humor gewesen, weil sie keinen

PORTRAITS FOR 'HORSE FEATHERS' (1932)
Harpo Marx

„Zitieren Sie mich mit den Worten, ich sei falsch zitiert worden."
Groucho

seiner Witze verstand und deshalb immer völlig konsterniert gewirkt habe. Trotzdem lobte er sie in den höchsten Tönen als „praktisch den fünften Marx-Bruder".

Chico erkannte man an seinem Koboldhut, seinem frechen Grinsen und seinem ganz offensichtlich unechten italienischen Akzent. Im Film wie im Leben war Chico ein liebenswerter Gauner, notorischer Glücksspieler und Schürzenjäger. Seinen Spitznamen, der „chick-o" ausgesprochen wurde, verdankte er der Jagd nach den „chicks", den Mädchen. Groucho zufolge war Chico immer an oder auf drei Orten zu finden: „Telefon, Pferd und Braut." In den Filmen setzte Chico seinen Alltagswitz geschickt ein, um Autoritätspersonen auflaufen zu lassen, zum Beispiel wenn er Groucho beim Pferderennen einen Leitfaden für Wetten nach dem anderen andreht, von denen jeder nutzloser ist als der vorhergehende. Chico hätte Groucho auch fast bei der Landversteigerung geschlagen, als er ihn mit seinen Wortspielen um das „viaduct" (Viadukt) aus dem Konzept brachte: „Why a duck? Why-a no chicken?" (Warum eine Ente? Warum kein Huhn?). Durch Chico, den einfachen und doch siegreichen Intriganten, „konnten sich die Einwanderer auf befreiende Weise an der amerikanischen Fremdenfeindlichkeit rächen, die ihnen das Gefühl gab, Bürger dritter Klasse zu sein", wie Raymond Durgnat schrieb. Selbst Chicos Art, beim Klavierspiel den rechten Zeigefinger auszustrecken, um die Tasten zu ‚schnippen', war raffiniert.

Harpo spielte die Harfe wie ein Engel und rührte damit seine Zuhörer zu Tränen, doch ansonsten benahm er sich oft wie ein kleiner Teufel und brachte seine Opfer zum Heulen – aus Verzweiflung. Sein Engelsgesicht konnte sich unter der Wuschelperücke und dem verbeulten Zylinder in das eines Ungetüms verwandeln, wenn er schielte und seine Backen aufplusterte. In einem Film kann ein Hoteldetektiv nur verblüfft zuschauen, wie eine Lawine aus gestohlenem Tafelsilber aus Harpos Ärmeln prasselt – einschließlich einer Kaffeekanne. In einem anderen Film durchsuchen ein paar Schlägertypen Harpos Manteltaschen nach gestohlenem Schmuck und finden stattdessen eine Fußmatte, ein Frisörschild, einen Schlitten, einen Eisblock und einen lebenden Hund. (Immerhin hilft Harpo aber auch einem Bedürftigen, indem er ihm anstelle von Kleingeld eine dampfend heiße Tasse Kaffee aus dem Mantel hervorzaubert.) In mancherlei Hinsicht glich Harpo einem ungezogenen Kind, das unablässig Vaterfiguren trotzte, wenn er anderen Männern beispielsweise ihre Zigarren, Krawatten und Rockschöße abschnitt. Bill Marx, Harpos Sohn, sagte einmal: „Mein Vater erlebte nie eine zweite Kindheit, weil er seine erste nie hinter sich ließ." Zum anderen war Harpo aber auch ein ewig lüsterner Faun, der sein Bein in die Hände von Damen wie Margaret Dumont legte oder hupend Blondinen hinterherhechelte.

Der Wahnsinn der Marx Brothers hat ganz offensichtlich Methode – aber steckt auch eine Aussage dahinter? Vielleicht drückte es ausgerechnet Harpo am besten aus: „Wenn dir alles über den Kopf wächst und du das Gefühl hast, die ganze Welt habe sich gegen dich verschworen, dann mach doch einfach einen Kopfstand. Und wenn dir noch etwas Verrückteres einfällt, dann tu es."

HARPO MARX

LES MARX BROTHERS : LES FOUS DU RIRE

Douglas Keesey

Pendant vingt ans, les Marx Brothers – Groucho, Chico, Harpo et parfois Zeppo – ont mis au point le tempo de leurs numéros dans des spectacles de music-hall et dans des revues à Broadway, avant de devenir l'une des plus talentueuses troupes de comiques du cinéma. Ensemble, ils ont tourné treize films de 1929 à 1949, parmi lesquels *Soupe au canard* (1933), *Une nuit à l'opéra* (1935) et *Un jour aux courses* (1937). On peut les voir aussi séparément dans des dizaines d'autres rôles au cinéma et à la télévision.

Groucho est instantanément reconnaissable, avec son gros cigare, ses sourcils broussailleux, sa fausse moustache en cirage et son buste penché en avant. Il incarne des figures autoritaires pour mieux en railler les côtés pompeux, sous les traits du capitaine Jeffrey T. Spaulding, du docteur Hugo Z. Hackenbush ou du procureur J. Cheever Loophole. Son frère Zeppo joue les faire-valoir, au service d'un Groucho toujours prêt au bon mot. Un jour, Groucho a même déclaré : « Il y avait un moyen infaillible de savoir si un nouveau gag marchait ou pas : c'était de le tester sur Zeppo. Si ça lui plaisait, on ne le gardait pas. » Même si, avec son beau profil et sa voix de ténor virile, Zeppo interprète les jeunes premiers romantiques, il finit par quitter la troupe au bout de cinq films, en disant : « Les faire-valoir, j'en ai soupé. » Une notice nécrologique le qualifiera plus tard ainsi : « Son point fort, c'était les blondes, pas les blagues. » Autre célèbre comparse au service de Groucho, Margaret Dumont joue, dans sept films, une dame de la haute société, soumise aux insultes et aux sous-entendus de Groucho : « J'aimerai pour l'éternité tout ce qui est « bon » en vous : vos bons d'achat, vos bons de réduction, vos bons du Trésor. » « Pourrais-je avoir une mèche de vos cheveux ? Vous vous en tirez à bon compte. J'ai failli vous demander toute la perruque. » Groucho a toujours dit que, si Margaret Dumont était la comparse idéale, c'est qu'elle arborait une expression de surprise permanente ... parce qu'elle ne comprenait aucune blague. Il lui rendit un très grand hommage en disant qu'elle était « pratiquement le cinquième frère Marx ».

Chico se distingue par son chapeau de farfadet, son sourire canaille et son faux accent italien. À la ville comme à l'écran, c'est un adorable arnaqueur, un joueur compulsif et un

PORTRAIT FOR 'HORSE FEATHERS' (1932)
Chico Marx

« Je cite : "J'ai été mal cité." Fin de citation. »
Groucho

coureur de jupons (« Chico » vient de *chick*, « nana » en anglais). D'après Groucho, « on savait toujours où trouver Chico : au téléphone, aux courses ou au lit, et pas tout seul ». Dans les films, les personnages débrouillards joués par Chico en remontrent aux autorités intellectuelles, par exemple sur le champ de courses, en vendant successivement à Groucho plusieurs guides des pronostics dont chaque exemplaire est aussi inutile que le précédent. Chico manque aussi de battre Groucho aux calembours, lors de la vente aux enchères d'un terrain, en faisant une blague malicieuse sur le mot « viaduc » : « Pourquoi un vieux duc ? Pourquoi pas un vieux baron ? » Intrigant modeste mais triomphant, Chico permet aux « immigrés de prendre une revanche libératrice sur la xénophobie américaine qui faisait d'eux des citoyens de troisième zone », écrivait Raymond Durgnat. Chico est malin jusque dans sa manière de jouer du piano, lorsqu'il tend l'index droit comme pour « tirer » sur les touches.

Harpiste séraphique, Harpo tire les larmes de son auditoire en arrachant à ses victimes des larmes d'impuissance, à force de les tourmenter par ses comportements de diablotin. Coiffée d'une perruque bouclée et d'un haut-de-forme fatigué, la face d'ange de Harpo peut se transformer en gargouille lorsqu'il gonfle ses joues et se met à loucher pour faire son *gookie*, sa fameuse grimace. Dans l'un des films, un gardien d'hôtel regarde, stupéfait et désemparé, une cascade d'argenterie volée se déverser des manches de Harpo, jusqu'à une cafetière. Dans un autre film, des voyous à la recherche de bijoux volés fouillent les poches de Harpo, mais n'y trouvent qu'un paillasson, une enseigne de coiffeur, une luge, un morceau de glace et un chien bien vivant. (Mais quand un homme dans le besoin lui demande un peu de monnaie, Harpo sort de son manteau une tasse de café bien chaud.) Harpo est un garnement défiant éternellement les figures paternelles, comme lorsqu'il passe son temps à couper les cigares, les cravates et les queues-de-pie de ces messieurs. Bill Marx, le fils de Harpo, affirme : « Mon père n'est jamais retombé en enfance, car il n'en est jamais sorti. » Bref, Harpo est une sorte de Pan priapique qui met sa jambe entre les mains des dames, comme Margaret Dumont, ou qui court après les blondes en actionnant sa corne.

La folie des frères Marx est évidemment très méthodique, mais véhicule-t-elle un message ? C'est à Harpo que revient la meilleure réponse : « Si vous en avez assez de tout, si vous trouvez que le monde entier est contre vous, marchez sur les mains ou faites les pieds au mur. Si vous pensez à quelque chose d'encore plus dingue, faites-le. »

PAGE 22

THE FOUR NIGHTINGALES (1908)

Gummo, Harpo, Groucho and Leo Levin in their favorite human-ladder pose. / Gummo, Harpo, Groucho und Leo Levin in ihrer Lieblingspose als menschliche Leiter. / Gummo, Harpo, Groucho et Leo Levin dans leur pose préférée, l'échelle humaine.

THE THREE MARX BROTHERS (1935)

2

VISUAL FILMOGRAPHY

FILMOGRAFIE IN BILDERN
FILMOGRAPHIE EN IMAGES

THE FOUR MARX BROTHERS

DIE VIER MARX BROTHERS

LES QUATRE MARX BROTHERS

PORTRAIT (1910)
Groucho (age 12) and Harpo (14) as boys standing outside their New York City apartment. / Groucho (12) und Harpo (14) in jungen Jahren vor ihrer New Yorker Wohnung. / Groucho (12 ans) et Harpo (14 ans), au pied de l'appartement familial à New York.

"We played towns I would refuse to be buried in today."
Groucho on their vaudeville days

„Wir sind damals in Käffern aufgetreten, in denen ich mich heute nicht mal beerdigen ließe."
Groucho über die Zeit beim Varieté

« Nous avons joué dans des villes où je refuserais aujourd'hui d'être enterré. »
Groucho à propos de l'époque du music-hall

THE FOUR NIGHTINGALES (1908)
Gummo, Leo Levin, Groucho and Harpo in their early singing act. / Gummo, Leo Levin, Groucho und Harpo bei einer frühen Gesangsnummer. / Gummo, Leo Levin, Groucho et Harpo, dans l'une de leurs premières formations de chanteurs.

"I attribute their success entirely to me. I quit the act."
Gummo Marx

„Ihren Erfolg haben sie ausschließlich mir zu verdanken. Ich hab die Gruppe verlassen."
Gummo Marx

« Ils me doivent tout leur succès. Je quitte la troupe. »
Gummo Marx

BELOW/UNTEN/CI-DESSOUS

POSTER FOR 'THE COCOANUTS' (1929)

The first big Marx Bros. movie was almost a silent film for United Artists, but luckily Paramount made it a talkie. / Um ein Haar wäre der erste große Spielfilm der Marx Brothers ein Stummfilm für United Artists geworden, doch glücklicherweise machte Paramount einen Tonfilm daraus. / Le premier grand film des Marx faillit être un muet pour les Artistes Associés. Heureusement, Paramount en fit un parlant.

RIGHT/RECHTS/CI-CONTRE

STILL FROM 'THE COCOANUTS' (1929)

When the bellboys demand to be paid, hotel manager Groucho asks them, "Do you want to be wage slaves?" / Als die Pagen ihren Lohn verlangen, fragt Hoteldirektor Groucho sie: „Wollt ihr denn Lohnsklaven sein?" / Aux grooms qui demandent à être payés, Groucho rétorque : « Pour manger, vous avez des pourboires ! »

F5-54

STILL FROM 'THE COCOANUTS' (1929)
Stuffy dowager Margaret Dumont is the perfect foil for Groucho to fool and offend. / Als spießige Witwe ist Margaret Dumont das perfekte Opfer für Grouchos Scherze und Beleidigungen. / En douairière collet monté, Margaret Dumont joue les souffre-douleur de Groucho.

STILL FROM 'THE COCOANUTS' (1929)
Overly friendly Harpo offers his leg rather than his hand to a startled bellboy. / Der übermäßig freundliche Harpo gibt dem verblüfften Pagen lieber ein Bein als seine Hand. / Le très familier Harpo tend la jambe plutôt que la main à un groom estomaqué.

"They were capricious, tricky beyond endurance, and altogether unreliable. They were also megalomaniac to a degree which is impossible to describe."
Writer S. J. Perelman on the Marx Brothers

„Sie waren launenhaft, sie waren so durchtrieben, dass man es nicht aushalten konnte, und sie waren alle miteinander unzuverlässig. Außerdem waren sie größenwahnsinnig in einem Maße, das sich unmöglich in Worte fassen lässt."
Schriftsteller S. J. Perelman über die Marx Brothers

« Ils étaient capricieux, retors à l'extrême et on ne pouvait pas compter sur eux. Par ailleurs, ils étaient mégalomanes à un point qui dépasse l'entendement. »
Le scénariste S. J. Perelman à propos des Marx Brothers

STILL FROM 'THE COCOANUTS' (1929)
For no particular reason, Zeppo and Groucho are about to fight Chico and Harpo. / Ohne ersichtlichen Grund brechen Zeppo und Groucho eine Auseinandersetzung mit Chico und Harpo vom Zaun. / Sans mobile apparent, Zeppo et Groucho provoquent Chico et Harpo.

"I am a Marxist, of the Groucho sort."
Anonymous revolutionary in Paris, 1968

„Ich bin Marxist, von der Groucho-Sorte."
Unbekannter Revoluzzer in Paris, 1968

« Je suis marxiste, tendance Groucho. »
Révolutionnaire parisien anonyme en 1968

STILL FROM 'THE COCOANUTS' (1929)
Groucho shows up at the party in a costume "condemned by *Good Housekeeping*." / Groucho erscheint zur Party in einem Kostüm, das „von Schöner wohnen für gesundheitsschädlich erklärt" wurde. / Groucho arrive à la réception dans un accoutrement stigmatisé par les magazines de mode.

PAGES 34/35
ON THE SET OF 'THE COCOANUTS' (1929)
Groucho, Chico and Harpo mug it up with the directors and crew, but some say Zeppo (third from left) was actually the funniest Marx brother in real life. / Groucho, Chico und Harpo grimassieren neben den beiden Regisseuren und der Filmcrew, doch einige behaupten, im richtigen Leben sei Zeppo (3. von links) der witzigste der Marx-Brüder gewesen. / Groucho, Chico et Harpo font les pitres avec les metteurs en scène et les techniciens, mais on dit que Zeppo (le troisième à partir de la gauche) était le plus drôle des quatre dans la vie.

Paramount
VOL. 13 SAT. DEC 6. 1930. No. 49
PARAMOUNT PRESENTS
THE MARX
IN
ANIMAL
WITH LILLIAN ROTH
DIRECTED BY VICTOR
BASED ON A MUSICAL PLAY BY GEORGE S. KAUFMAN, MORRIE RYSKIND BERT
AND HARRY RUBY.
SCREENPLAY BY MORRIE RYSKIND CONTINUITY BY
A Paramount TALKING Picture
Paramount Film Service Ltd.

STILL FROM 'ANIMAL CRACKERS' (1930)
Groucho's grand entrance as African explorer Captain Jeffrey T. Spaulding: "Hello, I must be going." / Grouchos spektakulärer Auftritt als Afrikaforscher Captain Jeffrey T. Spaulding: „Hello, I must be going" (Hallo, ich muss jetzt gehen). / Arrivée triomphale du capitaine Jeffrey T. Spaulding, explorateur de l'Afrique (Groucho) : « Bonjour, il faut que je m'en aille ! »

ADVERT FOR 'ANIMAL CRACKERS' (1930)
Like 'The Cocoanuts,' 'Animal Crackers' was first a Broadway play before being made into a movie. / Wie *The Cocoanuts* war auch *Animal Crackers* zunächst ein Theaterstück am Broadway, bevor es verfilmt wurde. / Comme *Noix de coco*, *L'Explorateur en folie* avait d'abord été une comédie à Broadway.

STILL FROM 'ANIMAL CRACKERS' (1930)
Harpo is doubly offensive: indecently attired and reckless with his shotgun. / Harpo ist doppelt anstößig: Er ist unzüchtig gekleidet und spielt leichtsinnig mit dem Gewehr. / Le double attentat de Harpo : à la pudeur et (presque) à la vie.

"When I started to write comedy, it was their influence that moulded my style. Sanity was out, logic was out, creative lunacy was in."
Spike Milligan

„Ihr Einfluss prägte meinen Stil, als ich anfing, Comedy zu schreiben: Vernunft war out, Logik war out, kreativer Wahnsinn war in."
Spike Milligan

« Quand j'ai commencé à écrire des comédies, mon style a été façonné par leur influence. Aux oubliettes la raison et la logique, place à la folie créatrice. »
Spike Milligan

STILL FROM 'ANIMAL CRACKERS' (1930)
Groucho first proposes marriage, then bigamy, and finally just wants to "sow a couple of wild oats." / Erst macht Groucho einen Heiratsantrag, dann schlägt er Bigamie vor, und am Ende möchte er sich nur „ein wenig die Hörner abstoßen". / Groucho demande le mariage, propose la bigamie, puis se contente de vouloir « batifoler ».

BELOW/UNTEN/CI-DESSOUS

STILL FROM 'ANIMAL CRACKERS' (1930)

Harpo's id is in overdrive as he gets a leg up on Margaret Irving. / Harpos lässt seinen Trieben mal wieder freien Lauf, und Margaret Irving bekommt ein Bein von ihm. / La libido de Harpo lui fait une belle jambe sur Margaret Irving.

LEFT/LINKS/CI-CONTRE

STILL FROM 'ANIMAL CRACKERS' (1930)

Harpo and Chico find that Louis Sorin's check bounces – literally, when they drop it on the floor. / Harpo und Chico finden heraus, dass Chandlers (Louis Sorin) Scheck „platzt" [engl. „bounce" = „springen", „ungedeckter Scheck"] – und zwar wörtlich. / L'argent que Louis Sorin remet à Harpo et Chico, sous la forme d'un chèque [en bois], leur « file » littéralement entre les doigts.

STILL FROM 'ANIMAL CRACKERS' (1930)
Chico and Harpo brawl at Margaret Dumont's formal dinner party, in a scene cut from the finished film. / In dieser Szene, die nicht im Endschnitt enthalten ist, prügeln sich Chico und Harpo beim festlichen Diner von Mrs. Rittenhouse (Margaret Dumont). / Chico et Harpo se bagarrent à la réception donnée par Margaret Dumont (scène coupée au montage).

STILL FROM 'ANIMAL CRACKERS' (1930)
Harpo: "I am the most fortunate self-taught harpist and non-speaking actor who ever lived." / Harpo: „Ich bin der glücklichste autodidaktische Harfenist und stumme Schauspieler aller Zeiten." / Harpo : « Je suis le harpiste autodidacte et l'acteur muet le plus heureux au monde. »

PAGES 44/45
STILL FROM 'ANIMAL CRACKERS' (1930)
Horn-honking, skirt-chasing Harpo uses a lollipop to lure a girl. / Mit seinem Lutscher lockte der hupende Schürzenjäger Harpo das Mädchen an. / Coureur de jupons et klaxonneur invétéré, Harpo appâte à la sucette.

PAGES 46/47
ADVERT FOR 'MONKEY BUSINESS' (1931)
Renowned humorist S. J. Perelman wrote the script for the Marx Bros.' first Hollywood film. / Der angesehene Humorist S. J. Perelman schrieb das Drehbuch für den ersten Hollywoodfilm der Marx Brothers. / Le célèbre humoriste S. J. Perelman est le scénariste du premier film hollywoodien des Marx.

THE MARX IN, MONKEY

The merry, mad Marxes are in again! The frenzied foursome that wowed the movie millions in "The Cocoanuts" and panicked them in "Animal Crackers" promise that "Monkey Business" will out-laugh and out-gross any Marx hit ever made. Groucho has a brand new crop of rapid-fire nonsense. Mute Harpo whangs the harp and chases the blondes. Chico, the tough guy, prowls his omniverous way. Zeppo furnishes the one sane spot in the lunatic Marxian universe. The buffooning brothers are invading an unsuspecting Hollywood for this opus.

BROTHERS BUSINESS'

The story is by Will B. Johnstone and S. J. Perelman, the nationally known humorists. It starts with the Marxes as stowaways on an ocean liner, with the whole ship's company in pursuit. Arrived in New York, they interview the ship reporters sent to interview them, then embark for Florida, by request. Having wrecked a millionaire's home, family and nerves there, Groucho psycho-analyzes a horse in his well known style. From there on it gets louder and funnier. Frank Tuttle will direct the Big Four of Fun, which is good news too.

STILL FROM 'MONKEY BUSINESS' (1931)
Something is fishy about these barrels containing shipboard stowaways Harpo, Zeppo, Chico and Groucho. / Irgendetwas scheint bei diesen Heringsfässern faul zu sein: Sie enthalten die blinden Passagiere Harpo, Zeppo, Chico und Groucho. / Ces tonneaux ne renferment pas des harengs fumés, mais des passagers clandestins (Harpo, Zeppo, Chico et Groucho).

Groucho: "I want to register a complaint. Do you know who sneaked into my stateroom at 3:00 this morning?"
Ship's captain: "Who did that?"
Groucho: "Nobody. And that's my complaint."
From 'Monkey Business'

Groucho: „Ich möchte mich beschweren. Wissen Sie, wer sich heute Morgen um 3 Uhr in meine Kabine geschlichen hat?"
Schiffskapitän: „Wer denn?"
Groucho: „Niemand! Deshalb möchte ich mich ja beschweren."
aus *Die Marx Brothers auf See*

STILL FROM 'MONKEY BUSINESS' (1931)
Harpo puffs out his cheeks to make his 'gookie' face as if he were a puppet in the Punch and Judy show. / Mit seinen Pausbacken tut Harpo so, als wäre er eine der Puppen im Kasperletheater. / Harpo fait son *gookie* (grimace inspiré d'un certain Monsieur Gookie) comme s'il était l'une des marionnettes du guignol.

Groucho : « Je veux porter plainte. Savez-vous qui s'est introduit dans ma cabine à 3 heures du matin ? »
Le commandant : « Non, qui ? »
Groucho : « Personne. Voilà pourquoi je porte plainte. »
Monnaie de singe

STILL FROM 'MONKEY BUSINESS' (1931)
Fake barbers Harpo and Chico first consider taking out a man's tonsils ... / Die falschen Frisöre Harpo und Chico überlegen sich zuerst, ob sie die Mandeln ihres Kunden entfernen sollen ... / Ces faux coiffeurs envisagent d'abord une ablation des amygdales ...

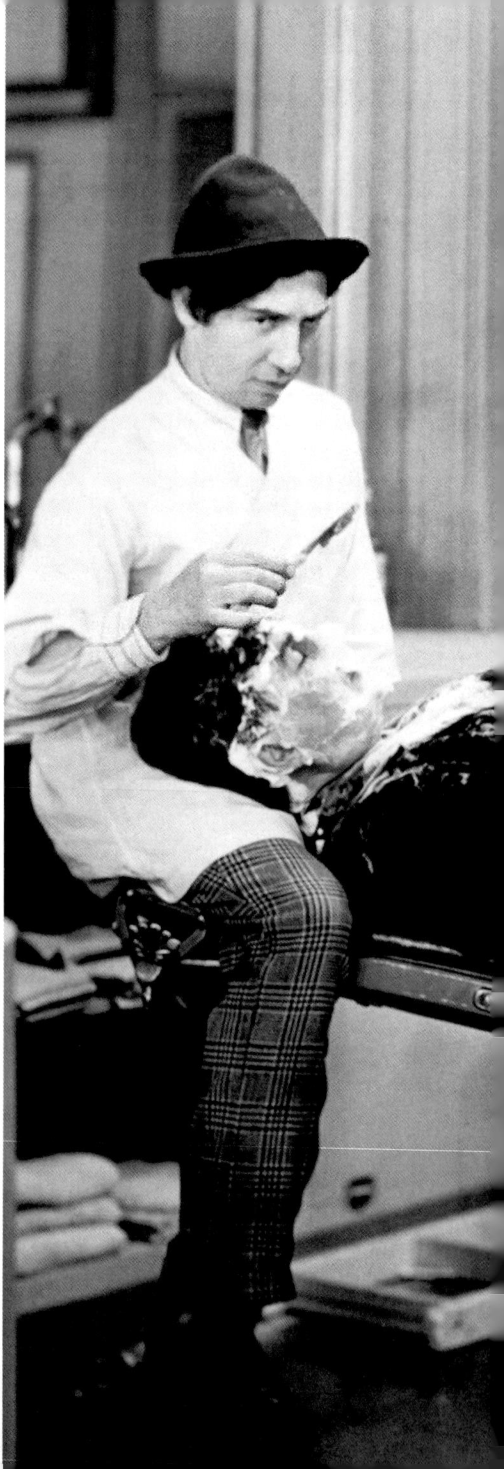

STILL FROM 'MONKEY BUSINESS' (1931)
... and then keep snipping away at the man's moustache until there is nothing left. This aftermath was snipped from the film. / ... und schnippeln dann so lange an seinem Schnurrbart herum, bis nichts mehr davon übrig bleibt. Das Nachspiel wurde aus dem Film herausgeschnitten. / ... puis coupent la moustache de leur victime jusqu'au dernier poil (moustache et scène coupées au montage).

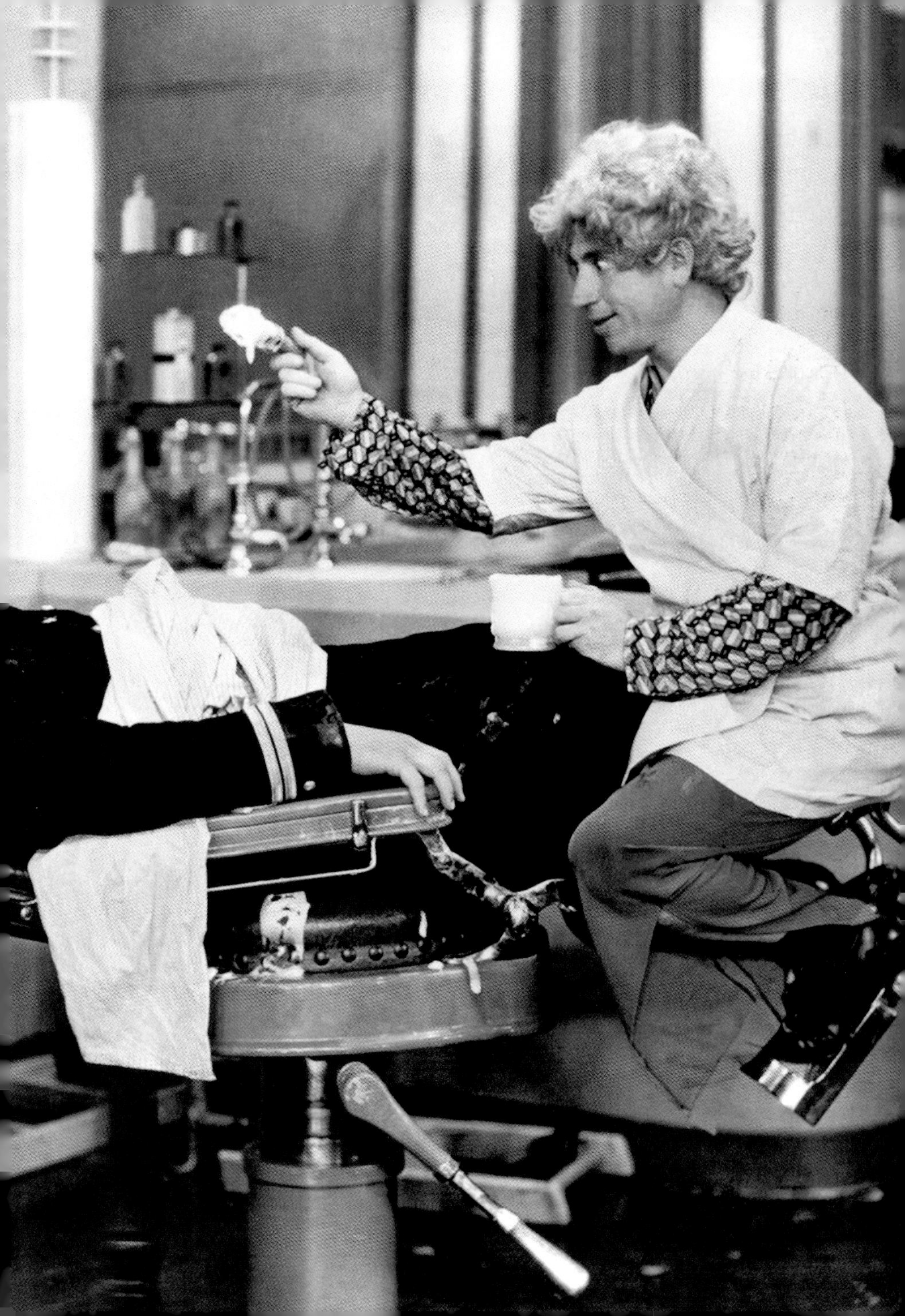

STILL FROM 'MONKEY BUSINESS' (1931)
His chess game disturbed, the cultured Harpo hits the offender on the head with his horn. / Weil sie sein Schachspiel gestört haben, schlägt der kultivierte Harpo die Bösewichte mit seiner Hupe auf den Kopf. / Dérangé dans sa partie d'échecs, le très civilisé Harpo sait donner un coup de corne.

"Now there sits a man with an open mind. You can feel the draft from here."
Groucho on Chico

„Da sitzt ein Mensch von großer geistiger Offenheit. Man spürt den Durchzug bis hierher."
Groucho über Chico

« Voilà un homme à l'esprit ouvert. Tellement ouvert qu'on sent les courants d'air. »
Groucho à propos de Chico

STILL FROM 'MONKEY BUSINESS' (1931)
Harpo tugs hard at this man's fake disguise – but the beard is real. / Harpo versucht mit aller Gewalt, den Mann zu enttarnen – doch der Bart ist echt. / Harpo a beau tirer sur le postiche, la barbe est bien réelle.

STILL FROM 'MONKEY BUSINESS' (1931)
Groucho enjoys the attentions of women who admire his manly tie, cigar and (greasepaint) moustache. / Groucho genießt die Aufmerksamkeit von Frauen, die seine maskuline Krawatte, seine Zigarre und seinen (aufgemalten) Schnurrbart bewundern. / Groucho adore les femmes qui adorent sa cravate virile, son cigare et sa moustache (en cirage).

STILL FROM 'MONKEY BUSINESS' (1931)
Groucho tells Thelma Todd: "I wish you'd keep my hands to yourself." / Groucho meint zu Lucille (Thelma Todd): „Ich wünschte, Sie könnten meine Hände bei sich behalten." / Groucho à Thelma Todd : « Vous ne savez pas quoi faire de mes mains, vous. »

SUNO
GLENDALO
PASADENO
GRIFFO PARK
TO LOS ANGLO
IF A NIGHTIN' GALE COULD SEENG LAK ZEP!
NEW LAND DEVELOPO
ROOFO GARDEN
HELP!
HELP
TRADE MARX
THE CHINKO THEATRO
ALL TALKO
BANKO
LAUGH CLOWNS
ZEPPO CULT
SELMO
CAHENGO
GROUCHO CULT
SHOOT TH' KEYS RESTURANT
SANTA MONICO
GASO
CHICO CULT
MELRO
GOLDEN HARPO EATS
PARKO 15¢
HARPO CULT
ZEPPO ST.
CHICO BVLD
O.K. GIVE MYSELF A TICKET
ATS A NICE-A SMASH UP. HEY, PARTNER!
CHASE ME
THE BLACK MUSTACHO CIGARS
STOPO
DING!
HONK!
ICE CREAMO
HOWDY GROUCHOS. HOW'S GAGS?
FINE LANGUAGE!
COPPO
GET IT?
GO ON, SHOOT AND PLEAD INSANITY!
STICK 'EM UP
Will By Johnstone HOLLYWOOD

STILL FROM 'HORSE FEATHERS' (1932)
Groucho as the new college president sings, "Whatever It Is, I'm Against It." / Als neuer Präsident der Universität singt Groucho: „Whatever It Is, I'm Against It" (Was es auch sein mag – ich bin dagegen). / Nouveau président de l'université, Groucho chante « Quoi que vous nommiez, je suis contre ! »

PAGES 58/59
STILL FROM 'HORSE FEATHERS' (1932)
Harpo is thirstier than the others. This scene was cut from the film. / Pinky (Harpo) ist durstiger als die anderen. Diese Szene wurde aus dem Film herausgeschnitten. / C'est Harpo qui a la meilleure descente (scène coupée au montage).

CARTOON FOR 'MONKEY BUSINESS' (1931)
Will B. Johnstone not only drew this cartoon for the pressbook but he co-wrote the film. / Will B. Johnstone zeichnete nicht nur diese Karikatur für das Presseheft des Films, sondern schrieb auch am Drehbuch mit. / Coscénariste du film, Will B. Johnstone est également l'auteur de ce dessin du dossier de presse.

DOG
1
CATCHER

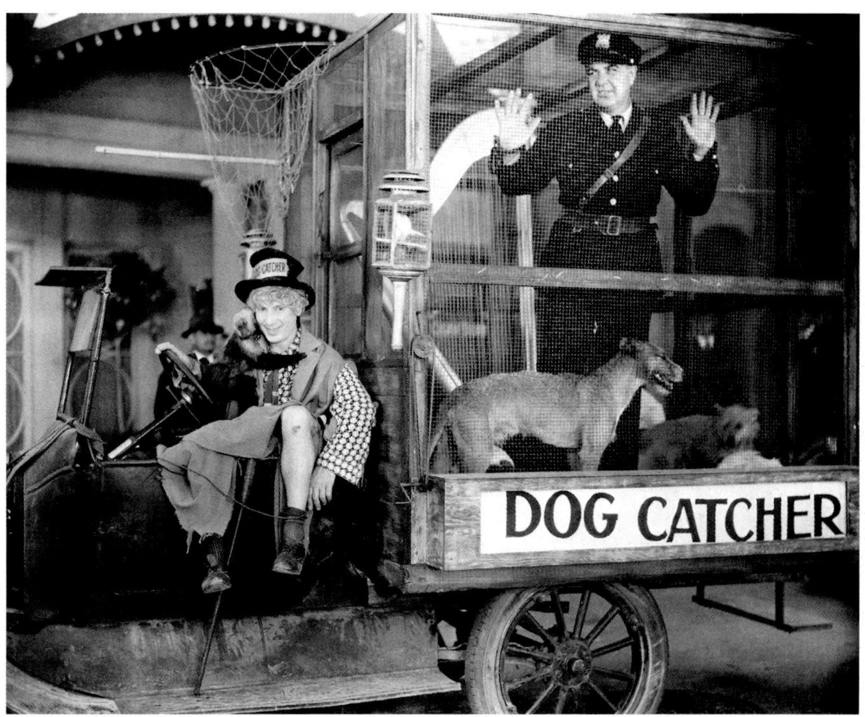

STILL FROM 'HORSE FEATHERS' (1932)
Dogcatcher Harpo has caught himself a 'police dog.' / Hundefänger Pinky (Harpo) hat einen „Polizeihund" gefangen. / Ramasseur de chiens errants, Harpo a trouvé un « chien de policier ».

STILL FROM 'HORSE FEATHERS' (1932)
Harpo shows why he is not impressed by the policeman's badge. / Pinky (Harpo) zeigt, warum ihn das Abzeichen des Polizisten wenig beeindruckt. / Harpo n'est pas du genre à se laisser impressionner par un insigne.

Professor Quincey Adams Wagstaff (Groucho) to his son Frank (Zeppo): "What's all this talk I hear about you fooling around with the college widow? No wonder you can't get out of college."
From 'Horse Feathers'

Professor Quincey Adams Wagstaff (Groucho) zu seinem Sohn Frank (Zeppo):
„Was hat es mit dem Gerede auf sich, dass du es mit der ‚college widow' [Nichtstudentin, die sich jahrelang auf dem Campus aufhält, um sich Studenten zu ‚angeln'] treibst? Kein Wunder, dass du nie mit der Schule fertig wirst."
aus *Blühender Blödsinn*

Le professeur Quincey Adams Wagstaff (Groucho) à son fils Frank (Zeppo) : « J'apprends que tu fricotes avec la "veuve de l'université" ? Pas étonnant que tu n'arrives pas à la quitter. »
Plumes de cheval

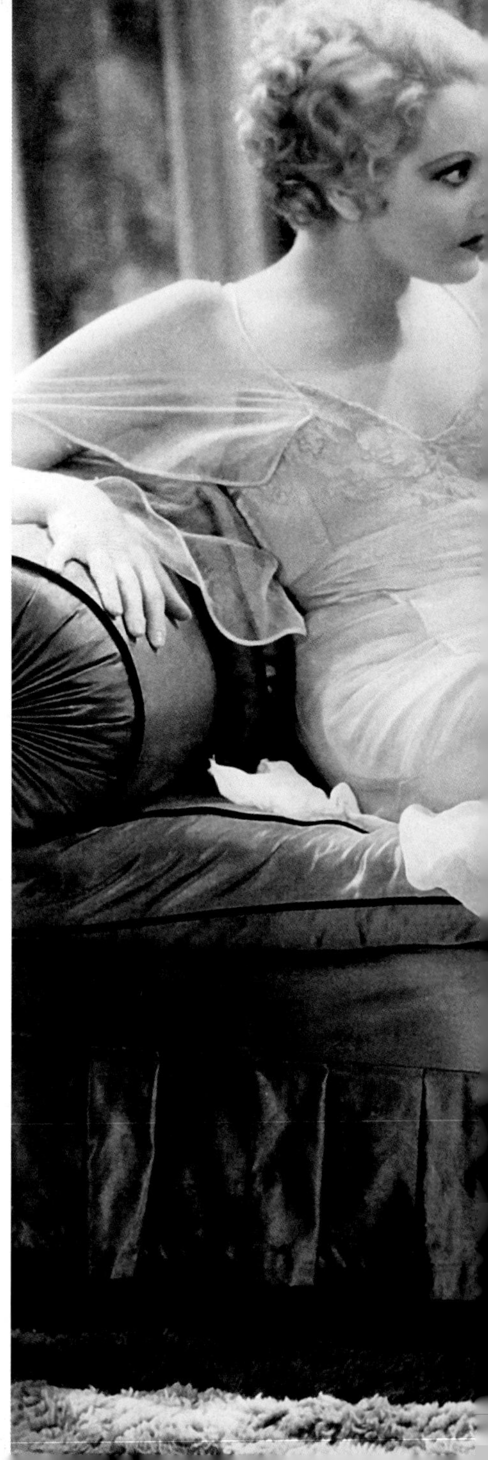

STILL FROM 'HORSE FEATHERS' (1932)
Harpo makes advances to Thelma Todd, but he is just pulling her leg in this cut scene. The Marx Brothers improvised a lot on the set, so many of the stills are from scenes and variations that never made it into the final film. / Pinky (Harpo) macht sich an Connie (Thelma Todd) heran, aber in dieser später entfallenen Szene will er sie nur auf den Arm nehmen. Die Marx Brothers improvisierten häufig bei den Dreharbeiten, und deshalb zeigen viele Standfotos Szenen oder Varianten, die es nicht in die Endfassung schafften. / Harpo veut séduire Thelma Todd, mais il ne fait que lui tenir la jambe (scène coupée au montage). Les Marx improvisaient beaucoup sur le plateau : de nombreuses photos sont tirées de scènes finalement coupées au montage.

PAGES 64/65
STILL FROM 'HORSE FEATHERS' (1932)
Stripped to their skivvies, Chico and Harpo act all embarrassed. Since when? / In ihrer Unterwäsche scheinen Baravelli (Chico) und Pinky (Harpo) ganz verlegen. Seit wann? / En caleçon, Chico et Harpo jouent les effarouchés. À d'autres !

KIDNAPPER

STILL FROM 'HORSE FEATHERS' (1932)
Harpo borrows a few garments from a lady in this cut scene. / In dieser entfallenen Szene leiht sich Harpo ein paar Kleidungsstücke von einer Dame aus. / Harpo aime tant la fourrure (scène coupée au montage).

STILL FROM 'HORSE FEATHERS' (1932)
In this wild game of football, Harpo (right) disputes the referee's call. / Bei diesem wilden Footballspiel ist Harpo (rechts) offenbar nicht mit der Entscheidung des Schiedsrichters einverstanden. / Harpo (à droite) conteste la décision de l'arbitre d'un match endiablé de football américain.

Professor Quincey Adams Wagstaff (Groucho): "Tomorrow we start tearing down the college."
Professor: "But where will the students sleep?"
Wagstaff: "Where they always sleep. In the classroom."
From 'Horse Feathers'

Professor Quincey Adams Wagstaff (Groucho): „Morgen fangen wir an, das College abzureißen."
Professor: „Aber wo sollen die Studenten dann schlafen?"
Wagstaff: „Wo sie immer schlafen: im Hörsaal."
aus *Blühender Blödsinn*

Le professeur Quincey Adams Wagstaff (Groucho) : « Demain, nous commencerons à démolir l'université. »
Un professeur : « Mais où vont dormir les étudiants ? »
Wagstaff : « En cours, comme d'habitude. »
Plumes de cheval

STILL FROM 'HORSE FEATHERS' (1932)
With his 'gookie' face and fake beard, Harpo looks like a horse's ass. / Mit seinem pausbäckigen Gesicht und dem falschen Bart sieht Harpo wie das Hinterteil eines Pferdes aus. / Avec son fameux *gookie* et une fausse barbe, Harpo déshonore la race chevaline.

MARX
BROTHERS
in A Paramount Picture
DUCK SOUP

STILL FROM 'DUCK SOUP' (1933)
Chico: "What is it got big black-a moustache, smokes a big black cigar?"
Groucho: "Does he wear glasses?" /
Chico: „Was ist es? Es hat große schwarze Schnurrbart, raucht große schwarze Zigarre?"
Groucho: „Trägt er eine Brille?" /
Chico : « Qui est-ce qui porte une grosse moustache noire et fume un gros cigare noir ? »
Groucho : « Il porte des lunettes aussi ? »

POSTER FOR 'DUCK SOUP' (1933)
A war comedy on the dangers of dictatorship, with Groucho bringing chaos to his country. / Eine Komödie über den Krieg und die Gefahren der Diktatur, in der Groucho als Rufus T. Firefly Chaos über sein Land bringt. / Dans cette comédie dénonçant les dictatures, Groucho mène son pays à la ruine.

STILL FROM 'DUCK SOUP' (1933)
Margaret Dumont: "I welcome you with open arms."
Groucho: "How late do you stay open?" /
Mrs. Teasdale (Margaret Dumont): „Ich heiße Sie mit offenen Armen willkommen."
Firefly (Groucho): „Wie lange haben Sie geöffnet?" /
Margaret Dumont : « Je vous accueille à bras ouverts. »
Groucho : « Et vous fermez à quelle heure ? »

STILL FROM 'DUCK SOUP' (1933)
Groucho: "Remember, we're fighting for this woman's honor, which is probably more than she ever did." / Firefly (Groucho): „Denkt daran: Wir kämpfen für die Ehre dieser Frau – und das ist vermutlich mehr, als sie jemals getan hat." / Groucho : « N'oubliez pas que nous nous battons pour l'honneur de cette femme. Elle n'a jamais dû en faire autant elle-même. »

"The first thing which disappears when men are turning a country into a totalitarian state is comedy and comics. Because we are laughed at, I don't think people really understand how essential we are to their sanity."
Groucho

„Wenn Menschen ein Land in einen totalitären Staat verwandeln, dann zählen die Komödie und die Komiker zu den ersten Opfern. Ich glaube, weil sie über uns lachen, ist den Menschen nicht klar, dass wir unentbehrlich sind, damit sie ihren Verstand nicht verlieren."
Groucho

« Ce qu'on supprime en premier quand un pays devient un État totalitaire, c'est la comédie et les comiques. Comme nous faisons rire, je ne crois pas que les gens se rendent compte à quel point nous sommes garants de leur santé mentale. »
Groucho

STILL FROM 'DUCK SOUP' (1933)
Groucho sings: "If you think this country's bad off now, just wait till I get through with it." / Firefly (Groucho) singt: „Wenn ihr glaubt, dass es diesem Land schon schlecht geht, dann wartet erst mal ab, bis ich damit fertig bin." / Groucho chante : « Si vous croyez que le pays est en mauvaise posture, attendez que j'en aie terminé. »

STILL FROM 'DUCK SOUP' (1933)
Chico: "Who you gonna believe, me or your own eyes?" / Chicolini (Chico): „Wem traust du mehr – mir oder deinen eigenen Augen?" / Chico : « Vous préférez croire qui ? Moi ou vos yeux ? »

"Take two turkeys, one goose, four cabbages, but no duck, and mix them together. After one taste, you'll duck soup the rest of your life."
Groucho's explanation of the title 'Duck Soup'

„Man nehme zwei Truthähne, eine Gans, vier Kohlköpfe, aber keine Ente [‚duck'] und vermische alles miteinander. Nachdem du einmal davon gekostet hast, wirst du für den Rest deines Lebens ‚einen Bogen um Suppe machen' [‚duck soup']."
Grouchos Erklärung für den Filmtitel *Duck Soup (Die Marx Brothers im Krieg)*

STILL FROM 'DUCK SOUP' (1933)
Chico and Harpo leap into bad guy Louis Calhern's chair just as he is sitting down. / Chico und Harpo werfen sich just in dem Augenblick in den Stuhl von Bösewicht Trentino (Louis Calhern), als dieser sich setzen will. / Chico et Harpo sautent sur le fauteuil du méchant (Louis Calhern) alors qu'il allait s'y asseoir.

« Prenez deux dindes, une oie, quatre choux, mais pas de canard, et mélangez le tout. Une bouchée suffira pour que vous fuyiez la soupe [anglais, to "duck" soup] pour le restant de vos jours. »
Groucho expliquant le titre du film *Duck Soup (Soupe au canard)*

SPECIAL EFFECT DEP'T

STILL FROM 'DUCK SOUP' (1933)
Groucho: "Sounds like mice."
Dumont: "Mice don't play music."
Groucho: "No? How about the old maestro?" / Firefly (Groucho): „Hört sich wie Mäuse (mice) an." Teasdale (Dumont): „Mäuse machen keine Musik." Firefly: „Nein? Wohl noch nie was von einem Maestro [‚mice-tro' ausgesprochen] gehört?" / Groucho : « Des pas de rats. » Dumont : « Les rats ne dansent pas. » Groucho : « Ah non ? Et les rats de l'opéra ? »

ON THE SET OF 'DUCK SOUP' (1933)
Zeppo helps Raquel Torres with her make-up. In the script she seduces him but the scene was omitted from the film. / Zeppo ist Raquel Torres beim Schminken behilflich. Laut Drehbuch soll sie ihn verführen, aber diese Szene wurde herausgeschnitten. / Zeppo aide Raquel Torres à se maquiller. Cette scène dans laquelle elle le séduit a été coupée au montage.

STILL FROM 'DUCK SOUP' (1933)
Zeppo and Chico shake hands in jingoistic joy as the country goes to war. / Zeppo und Chico schütteln sich in chauvinistischem Überschwang die Hände, als der Krieg ausbricht. / Zeppo et Chico se serrent patriotiquement la main à l'annonce de la guerre.

STILL FROM 'DUCK SOUP' (1933)
Singing satiric pro-war songs like 'All God's Chillun Got Guns.' / Beim Gesang satirischer Kriegshymnen wie „All God's Chillun Got Guns" (Alle Kinder Gottes haben Waffen). / Ils vont jusqu'à chanter des negro spirituals bellicistes et satiriques !

"I don't want to belong to any club that will accept me as a member."
Groucho's resignation from the Friar's Club in Hollywood

„Ich möchte keinem Club angehören, der mich als Mitglied aufnimmt."
Grouchos Kündigung seiner Mitgliedschaft im Friar's Club von Hollywood

« Je refuse d'appartenir à un club qui m'accepterait pour membre. »
Lettre de démission adressée par Groucho au Friar's Club d'Hollywood

nt's "Duck Soup" Four Marx Brothers Paramount's "Duck Soup" Four Marx Brothers Pa

VANILLA! They can't take it, but they thought Dewey could. The FOUR MARX BROTHERS as they repel a gas attack with Bicarbonate of Soda in PARAMOUNT'S "DUCK SOUP".

MARX
BROTHERS
in Paramount's
"DUCK SOUP"
Directed by
LEO McCAREY

STILL FROM 'DUCK SOUP' (1933)
Rufus T. Firefly (Groucho) to Margaret Dumont: "All I can offer is a Rufus over your head." / Rufus T. Firefly (Groucho) zu Mrs. Teasdale (Margaret Dumont): „Alles, was ich Ihnen bieten kann, ist ein Rufus [statt ‚roof' = ‚Dach'] über Ihrem Kopf." / Rufus T. Firefly (Groucho) à Margaret Dumont : « Sans vous, tout s'écroule. Avec vous aussi, d'ailleurs. »

ADVERT FOR 'DUCK SOUP' (1933)
The Marx Bros. go to war – in uniforms from different eras. / Die Marx Brothers ziehen in den Krieg – in Uniformen aus verschiedenen Perioden. / Les Marx s'en vont en guerre ... en uniformes anachroniques.

PAGE 84
PORTRAIT
The Marx Bros. suffered heavy losses in the Stock Market Crash, but they found work in films throughout the Great Depression. / Die Marx Brothers verloren einen großen Teil ihres Vermögens am Schwarzen Freitag, fanden aber während der Weltwirtschaftskrise Arbeit beim Film. / Les Marx perdirent gros lors de la Crise de 1929, ce qui ne les empêcha pas de tourner sans interruption.

NOTICE
POSITIVELY NO HELP
WILL BE HIRED AT THIS GATE
LEAVE NAMES AND TELEPHONE
NUMBERS AT THE CONSTRUCTION OFFICE
Metro-Goldwyn-Mayer Studios
BLONDES
WARDROBE
GAGS

THE THREE MARX BROTHERS

DIE DREI MARX BROTHERS

LES TROIS MARX BROTHERS

STILL FROM 'A NIGHT AT THE OPERA' (1935)
After Sig Ruman kisses Margaret Dumont's hand, Groucho will check to see if her rings are still there. / Nachdem Gottlieb (Siegfried Rumann alias Sig Ruman) Mrs. Claypools (Margaret Dumont) Hand geküsst hat, schaut Driftwood (Groucho) nach, ob noch alle ihre Ringe an den Fingern stecken. / Après le baisemain de Sig Ruman à Margaret Dumont, Groucho vérifie qu'il ne manque pas de bague.

"I was married by a judge. I should have asked for a jury."
Groucho

„Ich wurde von einem Richter getraut. Ich hätte auf Geschworenen bestehen sollen."
Groucho

« Je me suis marié devant un juge. J'aurais dû demander un jury. »
Groucho

STILL FROM 'A NIGHT AT THE OPERA' (1935)
In a sentimental scene, Kitty Carlisle comforts Harpo after he has been whipped by his master. / In einer rührenden Szene tröstet Rosa (Kitty Carlisle) Tomasso (Harpo), nachdem er von seinem Herrn ausgepeitscht wurde. / Kitty Carlisle réconforte tendrement Harpo que son maître vient de fouetter.

PAGES 88/89
STILL FROM 'A NIGHT AT THE OPERA' (1935)
A classic scene. Among those crowded into the ship's stateroom are maids, plumbers, a manicurist and a woman looking for her Aunt Minnie. / Ein Klassiker: Unter den Leuten, die sich in der Schiffskabine drängen, befinden sich Zimmermädchen, Klempner, eine Handpflegerin und eine Frau, die nach ihrer Tante Minnie sucht. / La foule de la fameuse scène de la cabine réunit femmes de chambre, plombiers, manucures et une femme qui cherche sa tante Minnie.

SHEET MUSIC FOR 'A NIGHT AT THE OPERA' (1935)

After five films, Allan Jones replaces Zeppo as the romantic lead and sings the love song, 'Alone.' / Nach fünf Filmen übernimmt Allan Jones von Zeppo die Rolle des Liebhabers und singt das Liebeslied „Alone" (Allein). / Au bout de cinq films, Allan Jones remplace Zeppo en jeune premier et chante *Alone*.

STILL FROM 'A NIGHT AT THE OPERA' (1935)

Acrobatic Harpo escapes from the ship's brig through the porthole. / Für den akrobatisch veranlagten Harpo ist die Flucht durch das Bullauge kein Problem. / Harpo l'acrobate s'échappe de la prison du bateau par un hublot.

STILL FROM 'A NIGHT AT THE OPERA' (1935)
Harpo's unconventional method of playing the trombone. / Harpo spielt die Posaune auf eher unkonventionelle Weise. / Harpo joue du trombone !

PAGES 92/93
STILL FROM 'A NIGHT AT THE OPERA' (1935)
Harpo, Chico and Allan Jones impersonate three famous Russian aviators. / Harpo, Chico und Allan Jones mimen drei berühmte russische Flieger. / Harpo, Chico et Allan Jones se font passer pour trois célèbres aviateurs russes.

PAGES 94/95
ON THE SET OF 'A NIGHT AT THE OPERA' (1935)
Director Sam Wood films the breakfast scene. Harpo has sugar on his face and ketchup on his lips. / Regisseur Sam Wood dreht die Frühstücksszene. Harpo hat Zucker im Gesicht und Ketchup auf den Lippen. / Sam Wood tourne la scène du petit-déjeuner. Harpo a du sucre sur la figure et du ketchup sur la bouche.

STILL FROM 'A NIGHT AT THE OPERA' (1935)
Chico (left) has found a way to keep the evil tenor Lassparri from singing. / Fiorello (Chico, links) hat einen Weg gefunden, den bösen Tenor Lassparri vom Singen abzuhalten. / Chico (à gauche) a trouvé un moyen de clouer le bec au méchant ténor Lassparri.

PAGES 98/99
ARTICLE FROM 'PHOTOPLAY' (FEB 1935)
The fifth Marx brother, Gummo, never made a film with his brothers, but eventually became their agent. / Der fünfte Marx-Bruder, Gummo, drehte zwar nie einen Film mit seinen Brüdern, aber er wurde ihr Agent. / Gummo, le cinquième frère Marx, ne tourna jamais avec ses frères mais devint leur agent.

Those Mad Marx

Editor's Note: With everyone going around saying, "Did you hear that one the Marx Brothers pulled in 'A Night at the Opera'?", we felt we just had to have a story on the Mad Marx Hares. Knowing from bitter experience that it was practically impossible to get any of them to remain in one place long enough to talk for publication, we sent our reporter to ferret out the fifth Marx Brother, Gummo Marx, who used to be in the act years ago, and is now associated with Brother Zeppo in his talent agency. Gummo's intimate revelations of the private life of the Marx Brothers follow.

"WHY is it," I demanded, coming straight to the bush instead of beating around the point, "that you Marx Brothers are nearly always together lately, except when you're apart?"

It was Gummo Marx to whom I put the question. Probably you have never heard of Gummo. You have never seen him on the screen and you never will unless he loses his reason. (Gummo has forgotten what his reason was, but he sticks to it just the same.)

Gummo is known far and wide, or at least wide, as the sane Marx Brother. In fact, Gummo is so sane that he quit the act fourteen years ago and went into the clothing business.

I had been told that Gummo was one Marx Brother to whom you could put an uncivil question and expect a civil answer. So here I stood in his Broadway office. The only catch was that Gummo didn't seem to be listening.

"Why is it!" I began again. But he checked me with a gesture.

Gummo remained silent while the cigar he was slowly swallowing traveled from just under the lobe of his right ear to just under the lobe of his left ear and back again.

Then he faced me without flinching, and answered fearlessly:

"Yes and no."

A moment later he was pacing the floor.

"Do you want to know why the Marx Brothers are always together?" he said, "I'll tell you why. Suspicion—intrigue—collusion! That's why. What has the career of the Marx Brothers become? An elimination contest!

"It's this way: I left the act and business immediately began to pick up.

"Zeppo left, and the new picture 'A Night At the Opera' is terrific. Now the suspense is terrific. Who will be next?

"That's what the boys started asking each other right after the preview. In fact, they all drew lots. Chico claimed his lots were under water, so he called the deal off. What Groucho called it is nobody's business.

"But someone's got to go. That's progress. Why, I can forsee the day when their pictures will be billed, 'Absolutely no Marx Brothers Whatever Positively!' And then won't they pack them in!"

"And what," I asked "are these brothers of yours really like?"

"So you want to know about father," said Gummo, reflectively.

I did not say I wanted to know anything about father, so Gummo began:

"It seems that one day he was sitting up in the balcony watching the boys down on the stage when two men in front

Hares

As Revealed by the Fifth Marx Brother to Edward R. Sammis

Caricature by Frank Dobias

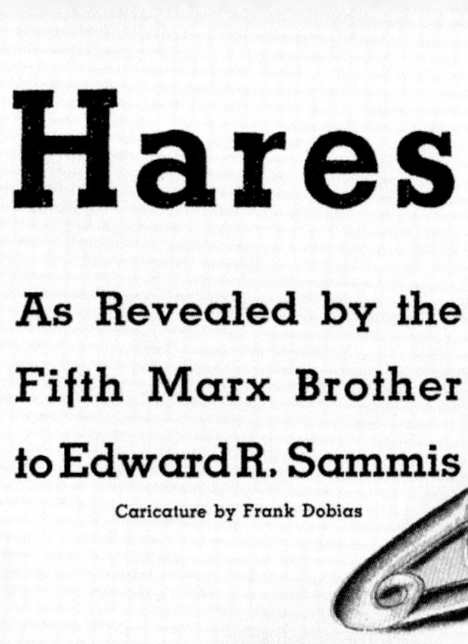

Those zestful zanies, Groucho, Chico and Harpo started life as acrobats and ended up in pandemonium. This three ring circus offers a brand new Marxian theory in the rakish hilarious "One Night at the Opera"

of him got to arguing about whether Harpo was really dumb or whether he could talk.

"The old man reached over and tapped one of them on the shoulder and said,

" 'He can talk all right.'

"The man turned around incensed.

" 'All right,' he said to the old man, 'I'll bet you ten dollars he can't.'

"My father looked at him with a gleam in his eye and said,

" 'What odds will you give me?' "

Gummo flicked six inches of ash from his cigar and continued: "You see how it was. We never had a chance to make an honest living. So there was nothing left for us to do but go on the stage. We started out as acrobats, building a human pyramid, but somehow we got off on the wrong foot, and our house of cards, (we never could decide who was the greatest card) came tumbling down."

"Very interesting," I said, "but what are these brothers of yours really — —"

"So you want to know how Groucho got his moustache," chuckled Gummo. "Well, that's quite a story. It seems that Groucho used to make up a moustache of crepe hair for every show. Then, one day, Harpo found a bald spot in his wig, just before curtain time. And he stole all of Groucho's crepe hair to patch it up. So Groucho had to go on with a moustache of burnt cork. But he made a tremendous discovery. Burnt cork didn't tickle like crepe hair. It changed Groucho's whole nature. He used to be gruff, glum and surly. Now he's impossible."

"True, no doubt true," I interrupted, "but what are these brothers of yours — —"

"I knew you'd ask that one," laughed Gummo. "Everyone does. Well, the way we got our names was this. When we were in vaudeville, there was a cartoonist, Art Fisher, playing on the same bill with us, who gave us those names.

"Where he got them, heaven knows. Of course, Harpo was playing the harp, but I'm sure that had nothing to do with it. Chico was a cheeky sort of guy—so what? Zeppo was playing a rube named Zep—pure coincidence. I, Gummo, was always gum-shoeing around—a happenstance. And then there was Groucho. He couldn't have been named for his disposition. Groucho isn't really like that. He's worse."

"Authentic, undoubtedly authentic," I nodded. "But tell me, what are these — —"

"Why did I quit the act?" [PLEASE TURN TO PAGE 89]

Discovered, Gummo Marx! Daffier than the others! He tells—with gestures—just how crazy they all are!

ARS GRATIA ARTIS
CAMPAIGN BOOK
THE YEAR'S BIG MUSIC, LAUGH AND GIRL SHOW
GROUCHO CHICO·HARPO
MARX BROTHERS
WITH ALLAN JONES
Maureen O'SULLIVAN
A DAY AT THE RACES
A Metro-Goldwyn-Mayer PICTURE

"If Groucho and Chico stand against a wall for an hour and forty minutes and crack funny jokes, that's enough of a plot for me."
Herman J. Mankiewicz, scriptwriter

„Wenn Groucho und Chico eine Stunde und vierzig Minuten lang vor einer Wand stehen und lustige Witze reißen, dann reicht mir das als Handlung."
Herman J. Mankiewicz, Drehbuchautor

« Si Groucho et Chico racontent des blagues marrantes pendant une heure quarante en restant appuyés contre un mur, ça me suffit comme scénario. »
Herman J. Mankiewicz, scénariste

CAMPAIGN BOOK FOR 'A DAY AT THE RACES' (1937)
Having gone to sea, to college, to war and to the opera, the Marx Bros. now go to the racetrack. / Nachdem sie zur See gefahren und in den Krieg gezogen waren, die Uni und die Oper besucht hatten, zog es die Marx Brothers nun auf die Rennbahn. / Après être allés en mer, à l'université, à la guerre et à l'opéra, les Marx vont aux courses.

STILL FROM 'A DAY AT THE RACES' (1937)
A classic scene: "Tootsie-fruitsie" ice cream vendor Chico cons Groucho into buying an endless number of worthless racing tip books. / Ein Klassiker: Der „Tuttsi-fruttsi-Eiscreme"-Verkäufer Tony (Chico) schwatzt Hackenbush (Groucho) unzählige Hefte mit wertlosen Tipps für die Pferdewetten auf. / Chico, le vendeur de glaces « Tootsie-fruitsie », pousse Groucho à acheter des tas de guides de pronostics sans valeur.

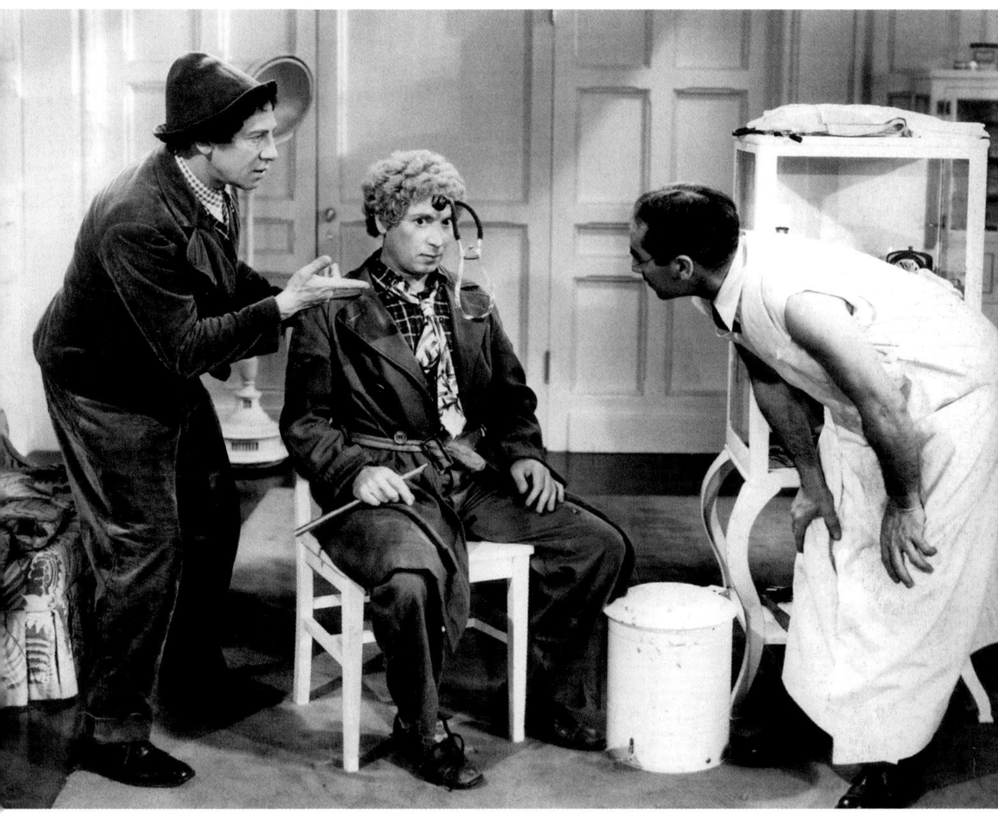

STILL FROM 'A DAY AT THE RACES' (1937)
Whatever ails Harpo, horse doctor Hugo Z. Hackenbush (Groucho) can't cure it. / Was auch immer Stuffy (Harpo) fehlen mag: Pferdedoktor Hugo Z. Hackenbush (Groucho) kann ihm nicht helfen. / Harpo est souffrant, mais Hugo Z. Hackenbush (Groucho), vétérinaire de son état, n'y peut rien.

PAGES 104/105
STILL FROM 'A DAY AT THE RACES' (1937)
Esther Muir baits a honey trap so that Groucho will be caught in a compromising situation. / Flo (Esther Muir) legt einen Köder aus, damit Hackenbush (Groucho) in flagranti erwischt wird. / Esther Muir appâte son homme pour compromettre Groucho.

PAGES 106/107
ON THE SET OF 'A DAY AT THE RACES' (1937)
Workmen Harpo and Chico will ruin Groucho's romantic tryst with Esther Muir by covering her with wallpaper. / Indem sie Flo (Esther Muir) eintapezieren, ruinieren die Handwerker Stuffy (Harpo) und Tony (Chico) ihr Stelldichein mit Hackenbush (Groucho). / Les peintres Harpo et Chico vont casser la baraque de Groucho en tapissant Esther Muir de papier peint.

TOMATO
JUICE

MGM

STILL FROM 'A DAY AT THE RACES' (1937)
Harpo adds insult to injury by making his patented 'gookie' face. / Stuffy (Harpo) macht sich mit seinem Pausbackengesicht zu allem Überfluss auch noch über das Chaos lustig. / Harpo donne le coup de grâce en faisant son célèbre *gookie*.

STILL FROM 'A DAY AT THE RACES' (1937)
In a scene cut from the film, Chico cools Esther Muir's amorous ardor by drowning her in wallpaper paste. / Tony (Chico) dämpft in dieser später herausgeschnittenen Szene Flos (Esther Muir) Liebesdrang mit einem Eimer Tapetenkleister. / Chico refroidit les ardeurs d'Esther Muir en la noyant dans la colle à papier peint (scène coupée au montage).

STILL FROM 'A DAY AT THE RACES' (1937)
Flute-playing Harpo leads black children in a song-and-dance number, now sometimes cut due to racial stereotyping. / Flötenspieler Stuffy (Harpo) führt eine Gruppe schwarzer Kinder bei einer Tanz- und Gesangsnummer an, die heute wegen der Rassenklischees hin und wieder aus dem Film herausgeschnitten wird. / Harpo et son pipeau mènent un groupe d'enfants noirs vers un numéro dansé, parfois coupé aujourd'hui pour cause de stéréotypes racistes.

Flo Marlowe (Esther Muir): "Why, I've never been so insulted in my life."
Hugo Z. Hackenbush (Groucho): "Well, it's early yet."
From 'A Day at the Races'

Flo Marlowe (Esther Muir): „Also, ich bin noch nie in meinem Leben so beleidigt worden."
Hugo Z. Hackenbush (Groucho): „Nun, es ist ja noch früh."
aus *Ein Tag beim Rennen*

STILL FROM 'A DAY AT THE RACES' (1937)
The Marx Bros. often aid a romantic couple, here Maureen O'Sullivan and Allan Jones, whose horse wins the race. / Die Marx Brothers helfen häufig Liebespärchen wie in diesem Fall Judy (Maureen O'Sullivan) und Gil (Allan Jones), dessen Pferd das Rennen gewinnt. / Les Marx viennent souvent en aide à un couple romantique, ici Maureen O'Sullivan et Allan Jones, dont le cheval est vainqueur.

Flo Marlowe (Esther Muir) : « Oh ! Je n'ai jamais été aussi insultée de ma vie ! »
Hugo Z. Hackenbush (Groucho) : « Vous êtes encore jeune. »
Un jour aux courses

NOW ON THE SCREAM!
. . . Broadway's most successful comedy hit! . . . The biggest laugh show in a generation! . . . A two-season sensation!...The movie rights cost more than any other play ever produced—and, measured in laughs, it was cheap at twice the price! . . .
ONE LOOK AT WHO'S IN IT—AND YOU WON'T LET ANYTHING KEEP YOU AWAY WHEN IT PLAYS YOUR LOCAL THEATRE!
MOVIE QUIZ $250,000.00 CONTEST PICTURES
THE MARX BROS.
PLEASE DO NOT DISTURB
madder than ever, with a million new gags... in...
"ROOM SERVICE"
WITH
LUCILLE BALL
ANN MILLER
FRANK ALBERTSON
RKO RADIO PICTURES
PANDRO S. BERMAN IN CHARGE OF PRODUCTION
DIRECTED BY WILLIAM A. SEITER
Screen Play by Morrie Ryskind

STILL FROM 'ROOM SERVICE' (1938)
Can Harpo, Chico and Groucho wake up this play with their Marxian madness? / Können Harpo, Chico und Groucho dieses Stück mit ihrem Marx'schen Irrsinn zum Leben erwecken? / Harpo, Chico et Groucho sauront-ils égayer ce scénario de leur folie marxienne ?

ADVERT FOR 'ROOM SERVICE' (1938)
Having started as a stage play, this is the only Marx Bros. movie not originally written for them. / Ursprünglich als Bühnenstück geschrieben, war dies der einzige Film der Marx Brothers, der nicht eigens für sie geschrieben wurde. / Cette pièce de théâtre transposée à l'écran est le seul film des Marx qui n'ait pas été écrit pour eux.

STILL FROM 'ROOM SERVICE' (1938)
A fake suicide note is pinned to Harpo's chest by a prop knife. / Mit einem Messer aus der Requisite wurde Faker (Harpo) ein gefälschter Abschiedsbrief auf die Brust geheftet. / Harpo arbore une fausse lettre annonçant son suicide.

"Outside of a dog, a book is a man's best friend. Inside of a dog, it's too dark to read."
Groucho

„Außerhalb eines Hundes [außer einem Hunde] ist ein Buch der beste Freund des Menschen. Innerhalb eines Hundes wäre es ja zu dunkel zum Lesen."
Groucho

« En dehors du chien, le livre est certainement le meilleur ami de l'homme. En dedans du chien, il fait bien trop sombre pour lire. »
Groucho

STILL FROM 'ROOM SERVICE' (1938)
Groucho, Chico and Lucille Ball mock the debt collector by giving him a "Hail and Fairwell" salute. / Gordon (Groucho), Harry (Chico) und Christine (Lucille Ball) verulken mit ihrem Salut den Schuldeneintreiber. / Groucho, Chico et Lucille Ball raillent un créancier en le saluant à la mode de l'époque.

PAGES 116/117
STILL FROM 'ROOM SERVICE' (1938)
Helping Frank Albertson to fake the measles (created by blowing iodine through a spaghetti strainer onto his face). / Die Brüder helfen Leo (Frank Albertson), Masern vorzutäuschen (indem man ihm Jod durch ein Sieb ins Gesicht blies). / Les Marx aident Frank Albertson à simuler la rougeole (grâce à de la teinture d'iode projetée à travers une passoire).

STILL FROM 'ROOM SERVICE' (1938)
Groucho, Harpo and Chico seem exhausted by their appearance in this not-entirely-successful hotel room farce. / Groucho, Harpo and Chico scheint ihr Auftritt in diesem nicht ganz erfolgreichen Hotelzimmerlustspiel ziemlich ermüdet zu haben. / Groucho, Harpo et Chico ont l'air épuisés par leurs rôles dans cette comédie hôtelière poussive.

PORTRAIT FOR 'ROOM SERVICE' (1938)
Harpo looks happy in the arms of Lucille Ball, future star of the hit TV series 'I Love Lucy.' / Harpo scheint sich in den Armen von Lucille Ball, dem zukünftigen Star der TV-Serie „I Love Lucy", recht wohlzufühlen. / Harpo heureux dans les bras de Lucille Ball, plus tard vedette de la série télévisée *I Love Lucy*.

STILL FROM 'AT THE CIRCUS' (1939)
... whereas Harpo and a live seal, both wearing badges, are permitted to board the train. / ... während Punchy (Harpo) und ein lebender Seehund, die beide Abzeichen tragen, in den Zug steigen dürfen. / ... tandis que Harpo et un phoque, tous deux munis d'un badge, ont le droit de monter à bord du train.

STILL FROM 'AT THE CIRCUS' (1939)
Chico (right) makes Groucho wait in the pouring rain because he doesn't have a badge ... / Antonio (Chico, rechts) lässt Loophole (Groucho) im strömenden Regen warten, weil er kein Abzeichen trägt ... / Chico (à droite) fait attendre Groucho sous la pluie parce qu'il n'a pas de badge ...

STILL FROM 'AT THE CIRCUS' (1939)
Harpo's expansive way of showing that he could be the next circus strongman. / Harpo zeigt sehr eindrucksvoll, dass er durchaus als Kraftprotz im Zirkus auftreten könnte. / Harpo est assez gonflé pour jouer les hercules au cirque.

"Writing for the Marx Brothers is an ordeal by fire. Make sure you wear asbestos pants."
Herman J. Mankiewicz to S. J. Perelman

„Für die Marx Brothers zu schreiben ist eine Feuerprobe. Du solltest dir vorher Asbesthosen anziehen."
Herman J. Mankiewicz zu S. J. Perelman

« Écrire pour les Marx, c'est l'épreuve du feu. N'oubliez pas votre combinaison en amiante. »
Herman J. Mankiewicz à S. J. Perelman

STILL FROM 'AT THE CIRCUS' (1939)
Interrogating the circus midget (Jerry Marenghi) in his miniature house. / Der kleinwüchsige Professor Atom (Jerry Marenghi) wird in seiner Miniaturwohnung verhört. / L'interrogatoire du nain du cirque (Jerry Marenghi) dans sa maison en miniature.

STILL FROM 'AT THE CIRCUS' (1939)
Groucho tries to shake money out of Eve Arden's bosom as they walk on the ceiling in suction boots. / Loophole (Groucho) versucht, Geld aus Paulines (Eve Arden) Dekolleté zu schütteln, während sie mit Saugnäpfen an den Schuhen an der Decke entlanglaufen. / Groucho veut faire tomber l'argent dissimulé dans la poitrine d'Eve Arden en marchant au plafond avec des chaussures à ventouses.

STILL FROM 'AT THE CIRCUS' (1939)
Harpo and Chico try to be inconspicuous when the strongman (Nat Pendleton) wakes up. / Punchy (Harpo) und Antonio (Chico) versuchen, sich unauffällig zu verhalten, als Goliath (Nat Pendleton) aufwacht. / Harpo et Chico tentent de passer inaperçus au réveil de l'hercule (Nat Pendleton).

ON THE SET OF 'AT THE CIRCUS' (1939)
Groucho and Chico sitting with legendary comedian Buster Keaton, who contributed gag ideas to this film. / Groucho und Chico sitzen mit dem legendären Filmkomiker Buster Keaton zusammen, der einige Gags zu diesem Film beisteuerte. / Groucho et Chico avec le légendaire Buster Keaton, qui leur donna des idées de gags.

STILL FROM 'AT THE CIRCUS' (1939)
Groucho to Margaret Dumont: "That night I drank champagne from your slipper – two quarts." / Loophole (Groucho) zu Mrs. Dukesbury (Margaret Dumont): „In dieser Nacht trank ich Champagner aus Ihrem Schuh – zwei Liter." / Groucho à Margaret Dumont : « Ce soir-là, j'avais bu du champagne dans votre soulier ... Un magnum ! »

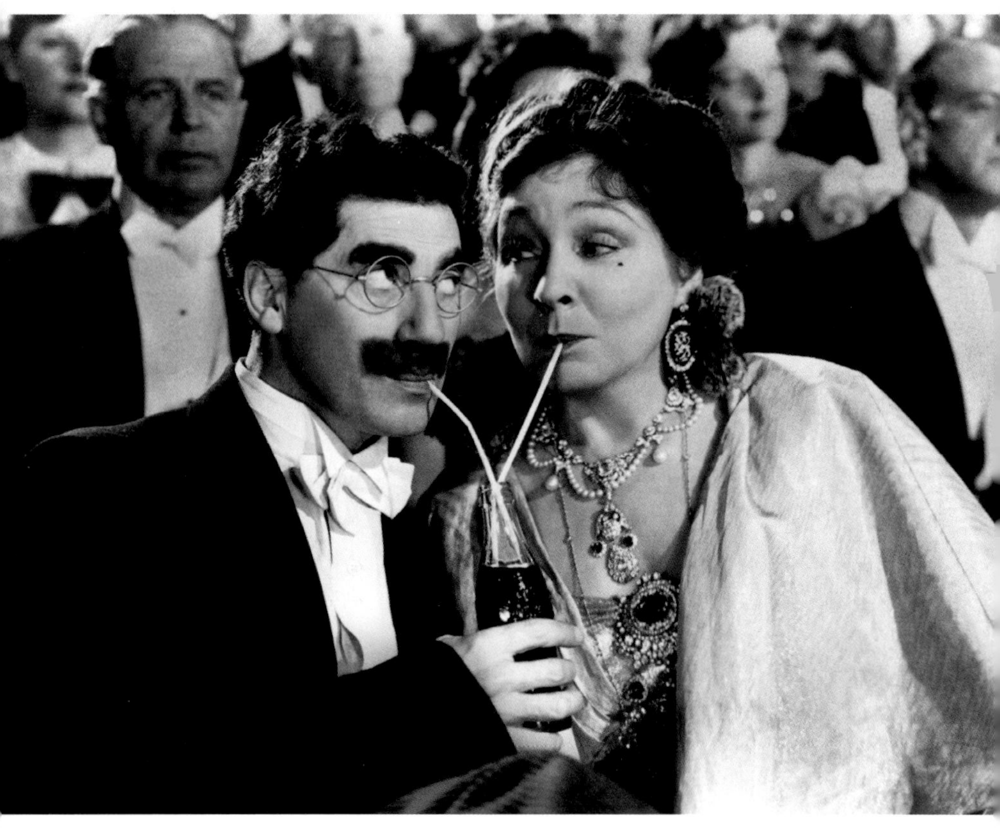

STILL FROM 'AT THE CIRCUS' (1939)
Uptight society matron Margaret Dumont in a rare moment of relaxed intimacy with Groucho. / Die ansonsten eher angespannte feine Mrs. Dukesbury (Margaret Dumont) in einem seltenen Moment der Entspannung mit Loophole (Groucho). / Margaret Dumont, la grande bourgeoise, dans un rare moment d'intimité détendue avec Groucho.

Susanna Dukesbury (Margaret Dumont): "You must leave my room. We must have regard for certain conventions."
J. Cheever Loophole (Groucho): "One guy isn't enough, she's gotta have a convention."
From 'At the Circus'

Susanna Dukesbury (Margaret Dumont): „Sie müssen mein Zimmer verlassen. Es gilt, bestimmte Gepflogenheiten (conventions) zu wahren."
J. Cheever Loophole (Groucho): „Ein Mann reicht ihr wohl nicht – es muss gleich eine ganze Versammlung (convention) sein!"
aus *Ein Tag im Zirkus*

STILL FROM 'AT THE CIRCUS' (1939)
When a giraffe licks her back, Margaret Dumont thinks it is Groucho being amorous. / Als ihr eine Giraffe den Rücken abschleckt, glaubt Mrs. Dukesbury (Margaret Dumont) an einen Annäherungsversuch Loopholes (Groucho). / Il suffit d'une langue de girafe pour que Margaret Dumont croie aux ardeurs de Groucho.

PAGES 130/131
PORTRAIT FOR 'AT THE CIRCUS' (1939)
In this publicity shot, it is Groucho (rather than Margaret Dumont) who is shot out of the circus cannon. / Auf diesem Werbefoto wird Groucho (und nicht Margaret Dumont) aus der Zirkuskanone abgeschossen. / Sur cette photo publicitaire, c'est Groucho (à la place de Margaret Dumont) qui jaillit du canon de cirque.

Susanna Dukesbury (Margaret Dumont) : « Sortez de ma chambre. Il nous faut respecter certaines conventions. »
J. Cheever Loophole (Groucho) : « Un seul type ne lui suffit pas. Il lui faut toute une convention. »
Un jour au cirque

EXIT

POSTER FOR 'GO WEST' (1940)
Having parodied the gangster genre ('Monkey Business') and the war film ('Duck Soup'), the Marx Bros. now take on the Western. / Nach ihren Parodien auf den Gangsterfilm (*Die Marx Brothers auf See*) und den Kriegsfilm (*Die Marx Brothers im Krieg*) nehmen sich die Marx Brothers nun den Western vor. / Après avoir parodié le film de gangster (*Monnaie de singe*) et le film de guerre (*Soupe au canard*), les Marx s'attaquent au western.

STILL FROM 'GO WEST' (1940)
A classic scene. Groucho (center) tries to make a fast buck off of Chico, but Harpo is faster. / Ein Klassiker: S. Quentin Quale (Groucho, Mitte) versucht, Joe (Chico) auszunehmen, aber Rusty (Harpo) kommt ihm zuvor. / Groucho (au centre) veut arnaquer Chico et le laisser en caleçon, mais c'est compter sans Harpo.

S. Quentin Quale (Groucho): "You love your brother, don't you?"
Joe Panello (Chico): "No, but I'm used to him."
From 'Go West'

S. Quentin Quale (Groucho): „Du liebst deinen Bruder doch, oder?"
Joe Panello (Chico): „Nein, aber ich hab mich an ihn gewöhnt."
aus *Die Marx Brothers im Wilden Westen*

S. Quentin Quale (Groucho) : « Vous aimez votre frère, hein ? »
Joe Panello (Chico) : « Non, mais je m'y suis habitué. »
Chercheurs d'or

STILL FROM 'GO WEST' (1940)
Thirsty Harpo's mouth is so dry that soon he will strike a match on his tongue. / Rustys (Harpo) Kehle ist so ausgetrocknet, dass er seine Zunge bald darauf als Reibfläche für ein Streichholz benutzen kann. / Harpo a la bouche tellement sèche qu'il pourra bientôt y craquer une allumette.

"It may be holy to you, Judge, but we have other ideas."
Groucho at his marriage ceremony

„Ihnen mag sie ja heilig sein, Richter, aber ich habe da andere Vorstellungen."
Groucho bei seiner Trauung

« Vous trouvez peut-être ça sacré, monsieur le juge, mais nous avons d'autres idées en tête. »
Groucho lors de son mariage

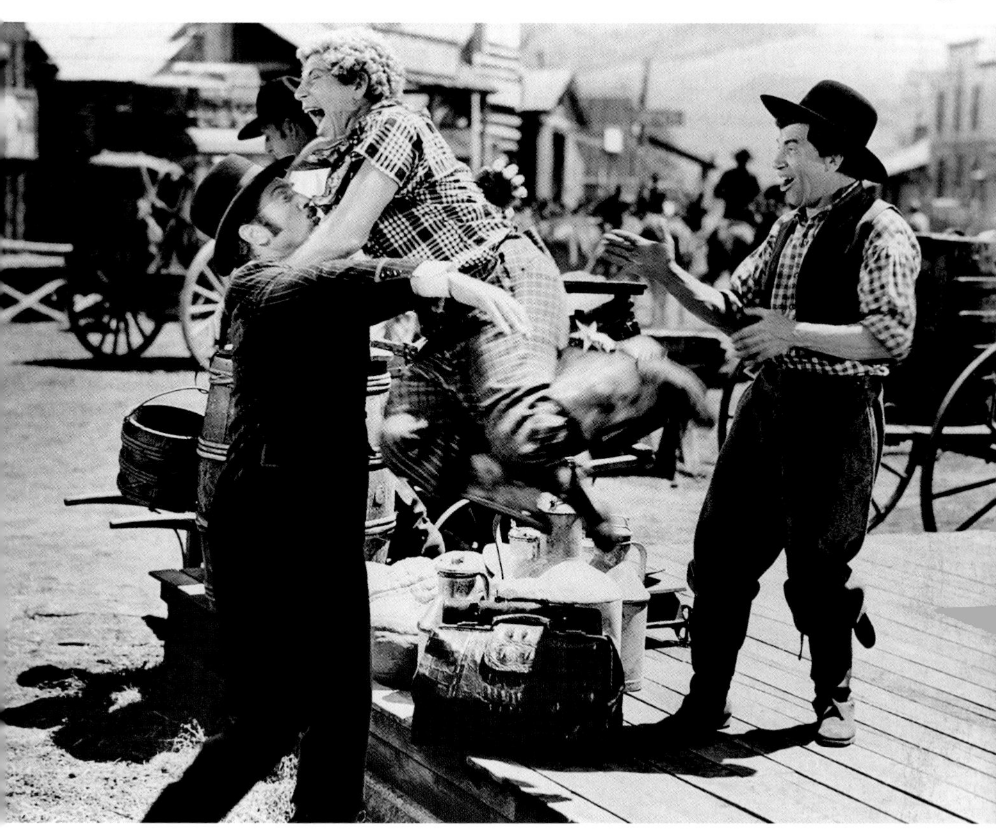

STILL FROM 'GO WEST' (1940)
Swindler Walter Woolf King didn't expect Harpo to be so easily or enthusiastically taken in. / Der Schwindler John Beecher (Walter Woolf King) hatte nicht damit gerechnet, dass sich Rusty (Harpo) so leicht und mit solcher Begeisterung übers Ohr hauen ließe. / L'escroc (Walter Woolf King) ne s'attendait pas à ce que Harpo se laisse avoir avec autant d'enthousiasme.

PAGES 136/137
ON THE SET OF 'GO WEST' (1940)
Filming the scene where villains have just sent Groucho to the bottom of the saloon stairs. / Bei den Dreharbeiten zu einer Szene, in der die Bösewichte Quale (Groucho) soeben die Saloontreppe hinuntergeworfen haben. / Sur cette photo de tournage, Groucho vient d'être expédié dans l'escalier du saloon par les méchants.

"I can
talk Indian.
I was born in
Indianopolis."

STILL FROM 'GO WEST' (1940)
Groucho: "White man want to make friends with red brother."
Chico: "And sister, too." /
Quale (Groucho): „Weißer Mann will schließen Freundschaft mit rotem Bruder."
Joseph (Chico): „Und Schwester auch." /
Groucho : « Homme blanc faire ami-ami avec frère rouge. »
Chico : « Et avec sœur ! »

STILL FROM 'GO WEST' (1940)
Evil Robert Barrat is faced down by gunslinger Harpo, who then pulls a clothes brush out of his holster. / Der böse Red Baxter (Robert Barrat) wird von dem „Revolverhelden" Rusty (Harpo) herausgefordert, der aber nur eine Kleiderbürste aus dem Holster zieht. / Harpo le flingueur défie le maléfique Robert Barrat, avant de dégainer ... une brosse à habits.

STILL FROM 'GO WEST' (1940)
Harpo's legs will elongate to an impossible length as he holds the train cars together. / Harpos Beine strecken sich auf eine unmögliche Länge, als er versucht, die Eisenbahnwaggons zusammenzuhalten. / Les jambes de Harpo vont s'allonger incroyablement pour garder les wagons accrochés.

"Those boys ruined my career! Nobody took me seriously as a dramatic actress. They always thought they saw Groucho peeking out from behind my skirt."
Margaret Dumont

„Diese Jungs haben meine Karriere zerstört! Niemand nahm mich als Charakterdarstellerin ernst. Sie dachten immer, irgendwann schaue Groucho hinter meinem Rock hervor."
Margaret Dumont

STILL FROM 'GO WEST' (1940)
On the out-of-control train, Chico yells, "Brake! The brake!" and Harpo breaks the brake. / Auf dem führerlosen Zug schreit Joe (Chico): „Brake! The brake!" (Bremse! Die Bremse!), Rusty (Harpo) aber versteht: „Break the brake!" (Brich die Bremse ab!) – und tut es. / À bord du train fou, Chico hurle « Tire le frein ! ». Harpo comprend « Retire le frein. »

« Ces messieurs ont brisé ma carrière ! Personne ne m'a prise au sérieux comme tragédienne. Les gens s'attendaient toujours à voir Groucho surgir de derrière mes jupes. »
Margaret Dumont

STILL FROM 'THE BIG STORE' (1941)
Chauffeur Harpo kindly holds the door for Margaret Dumont. / Chauffeur Wacky (Harpo) hält die Wagentür für Martha Phelps (Margaret Dumont). / En chauffeur bien élevé, Harpo ouvre la portière à Margaret Dumont.

Martha Phelps (Margaret Dumont): "But I'm afraid after we're married a while, a beautiful young girl will come along and you'll forget all about me."
Wolf J. Flywheel (Groucho): "Don't be silly. I'll write you twice a week."
From 'The Big Store'

Martha Phelps (Margaret Dumont): „Aber ich fürchte, wenn wir eine Weile verheiratet sind, kommt ein hübsches junges Mädchen des Weges, und Sie werden mich vergessen."
Wolf J. Flywheel (Groucho): „Reden Sie doch keinen Unsinn! Ich schreib Ihnen zweimal die Woche."
aus *Die Marx Brothers im Kaufhaus*

STILL FROM 'THE BIG STORE' (1941)
Wolf J. Flywheel (Groucho) is hired as store detective by Margaret Dumont, in her last film with the Marx Bros. / Wolf J. Flywheel (Groucho) wird von Martha Phelps (Margaret Dumont in ihrem letzten Film mit den Marx Brothers) als Kaufhausdetektiv angestellt. / Wolf J. Flywheel (Groucho) est engagé comme surveillant de magasin par Margaret Dumont, ici dans son dernier film avec les Marx.

Martha Phelps (Margaret Dumont) : « Je crains qu'après quelques années de mariage, une jolie fille surgisse et que vous ne pensiez plus à moi. » Wolf J. Flywheel (Groucho) : « Ne dites pas de bêtises. Je vous écrirai deux fois par semaine. »
Les Marx au grand magasin

ON THE SET OF 'THE BIG STORE' (1941)
Harpo and Groucho with director Charles Reisner, who had assisted on films by Charles Chaplin and Buster Keaton. / Harpo und Groucho mit Regisseur Charles Reisner, der bereits bei Filmen mit Charles Chaplin und Buster Keaton assistiert hatte. / Harpo et Groucho avec le metteur en scène Charles Reisner, ancien assistant de Charlie Chaplin et de Buster Keaton.

PORTRAIT FOR 'THE BIG STORE' (1941)
Harpo clowns around on the set with leggy costar Marion Martin. / Harpo albert in den Drehpausen mit seiner langbeinigen Kollegin Marion Martin herum. / Harpo rivalise dans le jeu de jambes avec Marion Martin.

PAGES 146/147
PORTRAIT (1942)
James Cagney joined Groucho on the intercontinental "Hollywood Victory" train to boost morale during World War Two. / James Cagney fuhr mit Groucho im „Hollywood-Siegeszug" über mehrere Kontinente, um die Moral während des Zweiten Weltkriegs zu stärken. / James Cagney et Groucho à bord du train *Hollywood Victory* qui traversa l'Amérique pour soutenir les troupes pendant la Seconde Guerre mondiale.

Man at hotel desk: "Sir, this lady is my wife. You should be ashamed!"
Hotel manager (Groucho): "If this lady is your wife, you should be ashamed."
From 'A Night in Casablanca'

Mann an der Rezeption: „Mein Herr, diese Dame ist meine Frau. Sie sollten sich schämen!"
Hoteldirektor (Groucho): „Wenn diese Dame Ihre Frau ist, dann sollten Sie sich schämen."
aus *Eine Nacht in Casablanca*

Le client d'un hôtel à la réception : « Monsieur, cette dame est ma femme. Vous devriez avoir honte ! »
Le directeur de l'hôtel (Groucho) : « Si cette dame est votre femme, c'est vous qui devriez avoir honte. »
Une nuit à Casablanca

STILL FROM 'A NIGHT IN CASABLANCA' (1946)
Chico (right) charging for camel rides: "Don't worry about the price. Whatever you got, I take." / Corbaccio (Chico, rechts) kassiert für Kamelritte ab: „Machen Sie sich keine Gedanken über den Preis. Ich nehme alles, was Sie haben." / Chico (à droite) indique le prix de la balade en chameau : « Dites combien vous avez, ce sera mon prix. »

STILL FROM 'A NIGHT IN CASABLANCA' (1946)
Charles Drake (left): "Marriage is impossible." Groucho: "Only after you're married." / Lieutenant Delmar (Charles Drake, links): „Ehe ist unmöglich." Kornblow (Groucho): „Aber nur nach der Hochzeit." / Charles Drake (à gauche) : « Le mariage est impossible. » Groucho : « Oui, une fois marié. »

STILL FROM 'A NIGHT IN CASABLANCA' (1946)
Nazi Sig Ruman's toupee will be sucked into a vacuum cleaner by Harpo. / Das Toupet des Nazis Heinrich Stubel (Sig Ruman) wird von Rusty (Harpo) mit dem Staubsauger aufgesaugt. / Le postiche du nazi (Sig Ruman) disparaîtra dans l'aspirateur de Harpo.

STILL FROM 'A NIGHT IN CASABLANCA' (1946)
This Rembrandt beauty inspires Harpo to play the 'Second Hungarian Rhapsody' on his harp. / Diese Rembrandt-Schönheit regt Rusty (Harpo) an, die Ungarische Rhapsodie Nr. 2 auf seiner Harfe zu spielen. / Touché par ce portrait de Rembrandt, Harpo interprète à la harpe la *Deuxième Rhapsodie hongroise* de Liszt.

STILL FROM 'A NIGHT IN CASABLANCA' (1946)
Sig Ruman attacks Harpo. This is the first film with Harpo's own hair, not a wig. / Stubel (Sig Ruman) greift Rusty (Harpo) an. Dies ist der erste Film, in dem Harpo keine Perücke trägt. / Dans cette scène où Sig Ruman attaque Harpo, ce dernier est visible - fait unique - avec ses vrais cheveux.

PORTRAIT FOR 'A NIGHT IN CASABLANCA' (1946)
Getting into the spirit of the 'exotic' locale (in fact, a Hollywood backlot). / Die Brüder bereiten sich auf den ‚exotischen' Schauplatz vor (der in Wirklichkeit ein Studiogelände in Hollywood war). / Ambiance « marocaine » (dans les studios hollywoodiens).

RIGHT/RECHTS/CI-CONTRE
PORTRAIT FOR 'A NIGHT IN CASABLANCA' (1946)
Groucho lounges lasciviously with Ruth Roman in a scene cut from the finished film. / Kornblow (Groucho) himmelt in dieser aus dem Film herausgeschnittenen Szene mal wieder lustvoll ein Mädchen (Ruth Roman) an. / Groucho et Ruth Roman se prélassent dans une scène coupée au montage.

PAGES 156/157
STILL FROM 'COPACABANA' (1947)
The woman behind Groucho's newspaper 'veil' is Brazilian bombshell Carmen Miranda. / Die Dame, die Devereaux (Groucho) hinter seiner Zeitung zu verstecken versucht, ist die brasilianische Sexbombe Carmen Miranda. / Le visage masqué par le journal de Groucho est celui de la vedette brésilienne Carmen Miranda.

STILL FROM 'LOVE HAPPY' (1949)
Groucho's comic cigar will outmatch all of assassin Otto Waldis' firepower. / Auch mit geballter Feuerkraft kommt Ivan (Otto Waldis) nicht gegen Grouchos komische Zigarre an. / Le drôle de cigare de Groucho aura raison de l'arsenal du tueur (Otto Waldis).

"You're only as young as the woman you feel."
Groucho

„Man ist nur so jung wie die Frau, die man fühlt."
Groucho

« On n'a que l'âge des artères des jolies femmes. »
Groucho

STILL FROM 'LOVE HAPPY' (1949)
Groucho as private eye Sam Grunion runs afoul of femme fatale Ilona Massey. / In der Rolle des Privatdetektivs Sam Grunion gerät Groucho an die Femme fatale Madame Egelichi (Ilona Massey). / Le détective privé Sam Grunion (Groucho) en froid avec la femme fatale (Ilona Massey).

STILL FROM 'LOVE HAPPY' (1949)
Marilyn Monroe: "Some men are following me." Groucho: "Really? I can't understand why." / Klientin (Marilyn Monroe): „Mir laufen ein paar Männer nach."
Grunion (Groucho): „Tatsächlich? Kann mir gar nicht vorstellen, wieso." /
Marilyn Monroe : « Je suis poursuivie par des hommes. »
Groucho : « Ah bon ? Je me demande bien pourquoi. »

ON THE SET OF 'LOVE HAPPY' (1949)
Screen sex goddess Marilyn Monroe makes an early cameo appearance in this film. / Marilyn Monroe, die spätere Sexgöttin der Leinwand, hat in diesem Film einen frühen Auftritt in einer winzigen Nebenrolle. / Marilyn Monroe fait dans ce film l'une de ses premières apparitions à l'écran.

STILL FROM 'LOVE HAPPY' (1949)
Harpo's version of a William Tell torture: point the gun at himself and eat the apple. / Harpo in seiner eigenen Version von Wilhelm Tell: Er richtet die Pistole auf sich selbst und verspeist den Apfel. / Guillaume Tell vu par Harpo : il se vise, puis mange la pomme.

STILL FROM 'LOVE HAPPY' (1949)
Critics were not kind to this film. Bosley Crowther: "Does anybody have any idea whatever became of the Marx Brothers?" / Die Kritiker hatten wenig Gutes über diesen Film zu sagen. Bosley Crowther schrieb: „Hat irgendjemand eine Ahnung, was aus den Marx Brothers geworden ist?" / Les critiques furent sévères, comme Bosley Crowther : « Est-ce que quelqu'un sait où sont passés les Marx ? »

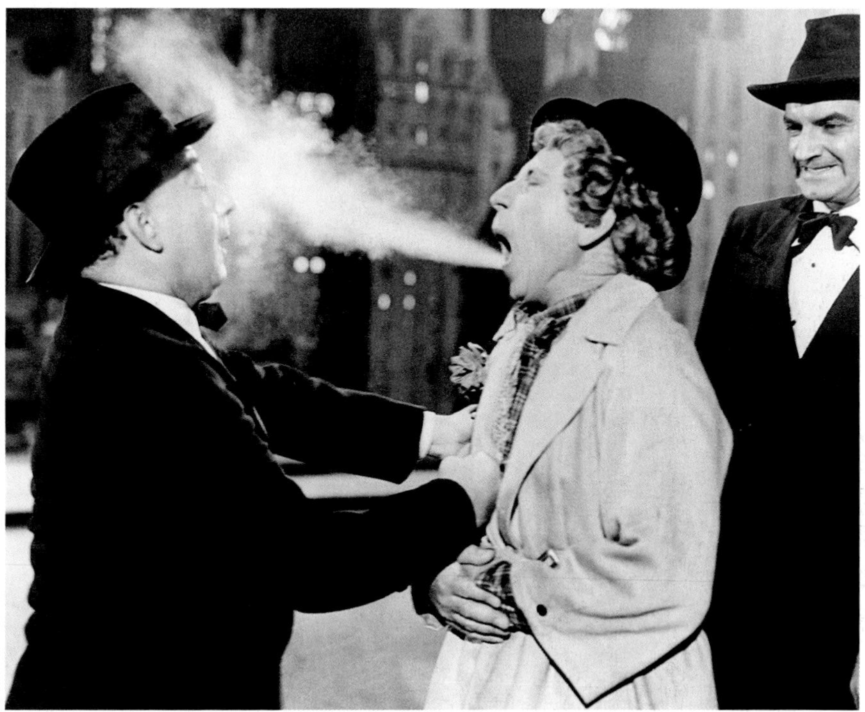

STILL FROM 'LOVE HAPPY' (1949)
Harpo blows smoke from a neon cigarette sign into the face of his adversary. / Harpo bläst den Rauch einer Zigarette aus der Neonwerbung in das Gesicht seines Gegenspielers. / Harpo crache la fumée d'une enseigne au néon pour des cigarettes au nez de son adversaire.

PAGE 166
PORTRAIT FOR 'WILL SUCCESS SPOIL ROCK HUNTER?' (1957)
With sex symbol Jayne Mansfield: Groucho's 40-second appearance in this film was a happy one. / Mit Sexsymbol Jayne Mansfield hatte Groucho einen sehr schönen Auftritt in diesem Film – auch wenn seine Szene nur 40 Sekunden lang war. / Avec la fameuse Jayne Mansfield, Groucho connut dans ce film quarantes secondes de bonheur.

ON THE SET OF 'LOVE HAPPY' (1949)
Harpo uses hotel bedsheets to improvise a parachute in the rooftop chase sequence. / Harpo benutzt die Bettlaken aus dem Hotel in dieser Verfolgungsjagd als Fallschirm. / Dans la poursuite sur les toits, Harpo se fait un parachute avec des draps.

LATER DAYS

DIE ZEIT DANACH

LES DERNIERS FILMS

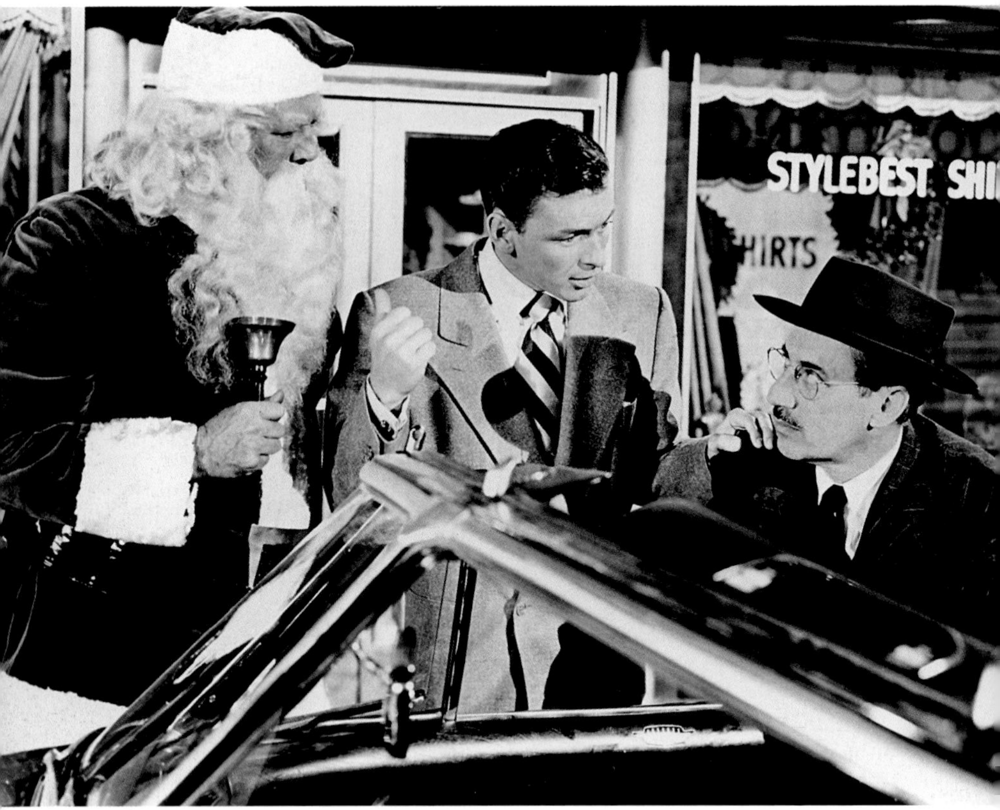

STILL FROM 'DOUBLE DYNAMITE' (1951)
Best known for its show-stopping duet, 'It's Only Money,' sung by Frank Sinatra and Groucho. / Die bekannteste Nummer dieses Films war das mitreißende Duett „It's Only Money" (Es ist bloß Geld), gesungen von Frank Sinatra und Groucho. / Le clou de ce film est la chanson *It's Only Money*, interprétée par Frank Sinatra et Groucho.

"I find television very educating. Every time somebody turns on the set, I go into the other room and read a book."
Groucho

„Ich finde, dass Fernsehen bildet. Jedes Mal, wenn jemand die Kiste anschaltet, geh ich ins andere Zimmer und lese ein Buch."
Groucho

« C'est très instructif, la télévision. Dès que quelqu'un l'allume, je change de pièce et je prends un livre. »
Groucho

STILL FROM 'A GIRL IN EVERY PORT' (1952)
Groucho and William Bendix as sailors vying for the love of waitress Marie Wilson. / Groucho und William Bendix spielen zwei Matrosen, die beide um die Liebe der Kellnerin Jane (Marie Wilson) buhlen. / Deux marins (Groucho et William Bendix) se disputent les faveurs d'une seule serveuse (Marie Wilson).

STILL FROM 'THE STORY OF MANKIND' (1957)
Harpo as Sir Isaac Newton is struck by the idea of gravity. / Harpo entdeckt als Sir Isaac Newton das Gesetz der Schwerkraft. / Isaac Newton, sous les traits de Harpo, découvre les fruits de la pesanteur.

STILL FROM 'THE STORY OF MANKIND' (1957)
Chico as a skeptical monk (right) listens to Christopher Columbus (Anthony Dexter) explain that the world is round. / Chico (rechts) lauscht als skeptischer Mönch, wie ihm Kolumbus (Anthony Dexter) erklärt, dass die Welt eine Kugel sei. / Un moine sceptique (Chico) écoute Christophe Colomb (Anthony Dexter) lui expliquer que la terre est ronde.

"This is what I want on my tombstone: Here lies Groucho Marx, and lies and lies and lies."
Groucho

„Auf meinem Grabstein soll stehen: ‚Here lies Groucho Marx, and lies and lies and lies.' [Hier liegt/lügt Groucho Marx und lügt und lügt und lügt.]"
Groucho

« Voici ce que je veux comme épitaphe : "Ci-gît Groucho Marx éternellement … éternel menteur devant l'Éternel." »
Groucho

PORTRAIT FOR 'THE MIKADO' (1960) (TV)
... as Ko-Ko, the Lord High Executioner, in this comic opera. / ... als Oberhofhenker Ko-Ko in dieser komischen Operette. / ... celui de Ko-Ko, le chambellan du seigneur, dans cette opérette comique.

PORTRAIT FOR 'THE MIKADO' (1960) (TV)
Groucho's lifelong passion for Gilbert and Sullivan finally resulted in a starring role ... / Grouchos lebenslange Bewunderung für Gilbert und Sullivan bescherte ihm schließlich diese Rolle ... / La passion de Groucho pour les œuvres de Gilbert et Sullivan récompensée par un grand rôle ...

STILL FROM 'SKIDOO' (1968)
Groucho as a gangster "God" converted to peace and love with Alexandra Hay. / Groucho als „Gott", der von Darlene Banks (Alexandra Hay) „bekehrt" und auf den rechten Weg zurückgeführt wird. / Auprès d'Alexandra Hay, Groucho dans le rôle de « Dieu », parrain de la pègre reconverti en hippie.

PORTRAIT FOR 'SKIDOO' (1968)
Groucho: "I played 'God.' Jesus, I hope God doesn't look like that." / Groucho: „Ich habe ‚Gott' gespielt. Jesus, ich hoffe, Gott sieht anders aus." / Groucho : « J'ai été "Dieu" à l'écran. Doux Jésus, j'espère que Dieu ne ressemble pas à ça ! »

PAGES 176/177
PORTRAIT (1958)
Harpo, Zeppo, Chico, Groucho and Gummo in one of their last photographs together. / Harpo, Zeppo, Chico, Groucho und Gummo auf einem ihrer letzten gemeinsamen Fotos. / Harpo, Zeppo, Chico, Groucho et Gummo réunis pour l'une des toutes dernières fois.

PAGE 178
PORTRAIT FOR 'SKIDOO' (1968)

3

CHRONOLOGY

CHRONOLOGIE

CHRONOLOGIE

CHRONOLOGY

22 March 1887 Leonard (Chico) Marx born in New York City to Jewish immigrant parents, Simon (Sam or "Frenchie") and Miene (Minnie).

23 November 1888 Adolph (Harpo) Marx born.

2 October 1890 Julius (Groucho) Marx born.

23 October 1892 Milton (Gummo) Marx born.

25 February 1901 Herbert (Zeppo) Marx born.

1907 Groucho and Gummo begin to tour in vaudeville acts and are joined by Harpo (1908) and Chico (1912). Zeppo replaces Gummo in 1918.

1920 The Marx Brothers make their movie debut in *Humorisk*, a lost silent short.

1924 Broadway comedy revue *I'll Say She Is* is lauded by influential theatre critic Alexander Woollcott.

1925–1927 *The Cocoanuts*, a successful musical comedy play, is followed by the stage show of *Animal Crackers* (1928).

1929 First feature-length film, *The Cocoanuts*.

1931 Move to Hollywood and make *Monkey Business*.

1932 On the cover of *Time* magazine as a comedy phenomenon.

1933 *Duck Soup* bombs at the box office.

1934 Tired of playing the straight man, Zeppo leaves the Marx Brothers' act.

1935 *A Night at the Opera*, the first Marx Brothers film for producer Irving Thalberg at MGM, is a tremendous critical and commercial success. Before the film is shot, its jokes are audience-tested and honed during a road tour.

1936 Salvador Dalí writes an (unfilmed) screenplay for them and sends Harpo a harp strung with barbed wire.

1947 Groucho hosts a radio quiz show, *You Bet Your Life*, which moves to television (1950–1961).

1949 *Love Happy* is their last film as a team.

1959 Make their last television appearance together in 'The Incredible Jewel Robbery,' an episode of *General Electric Theater*. Groucho publishes autobiography, *Groucho and Me*, followed by *Memoirs of a Mangy Lover* (1963) and *The Groucho Letters* (1967).

1961 Harpo publishes autobiography, *Harpo Speaks!* Chico dies on 11 October.

28 September 1964 Harpo dies.

1972 Groucho is made Commandeur dans l'Ordre des Arts et des Lettres by the French government at the Cannes Film Festival.

1974 Groucho receives an Honorary Oscar at the Academy Awards in recognition of his brilliant creativity.

1977 Groucho, Harpo, Chico and Zeppo are inducted into the Hollywood Hall of Fame. Gummo dies on 21 April. Groucho dies on 19 August.

30 November 1979 Zeppo dies.

1998 The American Film Institute names *Duck Soup* as one of the 100 Greatest American Movies of All Time.

MARIE DRESSLER & HARPO MARX

CHRONOLOGIE

22. März 1887 Leonard (Chico) Marx wird in New York als Sohn der jüdischen Einwanderer Simon (Sam oder auch „Frenchie" genannt) und Miene (Minnie) Marx geboren.

23. November 1888 Adolph (Harpo) Marx kommt zur Welt.

2. Oktober 1890 Julius (Groucho) Marx kommt zur Welt.

23. Oktober 1892 Milton (Gummo) Marx kommt zur Welt.

25. Februar 1901 Herbert (Zeppo) Marx kommt zur Welt.

1907 Groucho und Gummo beginnen, mit Varietenummern aufzutreten. Später gesellen sich auch Harpo (1908) und Chico (1912) dazu. Zeppo tritt 1918 an die Stelle von Gummo.

1920 Die Marx Brothers feiern ihr Leinwanddebüt mit *Humorisk*, einem kurzen, mittlerweile verschollenen Stummfilm.

1924 Der einflussreiche Theaterkritiker Alexander Woolcott lobt die komische Broadwayrevue *I'll Say She Is*.

1925–1927 Auf die erfolgreiche Musikkomödie The Cocoanuts folgt die Bühnenshow *Animal Crackers* (1928).

1929 Der erste abendfüllende Spielfilm ist *The Cocoanuts (Cocoanuts)*.

1931 Die Marx Brothers ziehen nach Hollywood und drehen *Monkey Business (Die Marx Brothers auf See/Affentheater)*.

1932 Sie landen als komödiantisches Phänomen auf dem Titelbild des Nachrichtenmagazins *Time*.

1933 *Duck Soup (Die Marx Brothers im Krieg)* fällt beim Publikum völlig durch.

1934 Zeppo ist es leid, den ehrbaren Kerl zu spielen, und verlässt die Marx Brothers.

1935 *A Night at the Opera (Die Marx Brothers in der Oper/Skandal in der Oper)*, der erste Film der Marx Brothers für Produzent Irving Thalberg bei MGM, wird zu einem ungeheuren Erfolg bei den Kritikern wie auch an den Kinokassen. Vor den Dreharbeiten wurden die Gags vor Publikum getestet und während einer Tournee geschliffen.

1936 Salvador Dalí schreibt ein (nie verfilmtes) Drehbuch für sie und schickt Harpo eine mit Stacheldraht bespannte Harfe.

1947 Groucho moderiert das Ratespiel *You Bet Your Life*, zuerst im Rundfunk und später im Fernsehen (1950-1961).

1949 *Love Happy (Die Marx Brothers im Theater/Glücklich verliebt)* ist der letzte gemeinsame Film der Marx Brothers.

1959 In der Folge „The Incredible Jewel Robbery" aus der Reihe *General Electric Theater* treten sie zum letzten Mal gemeinsam im Fernsehen auf. Groucho veröffentlicht seine Autobiografie, *Groucho and Me (Schule des Lächelns/Groucho und ich)*, gefolgt von *Memoirs of a Mangy Lover* (*Memoiren eines spitzen Lumpen*, 1963) und *The Groucho Letters* (*Die Groucho-Letters*, 1967).

1961 Harpo veröffentlicht seine Autobiografie, *Harpo Speaks! (Harpo spricht)*. Chico stirbt am 11. Oktober.

28. September 1964 Harpo stirbt.

1972 Groucho wird während des Filmfestivals in Cannes von der französischen Regierung zum „Commandeur dans l'Ordre des Arts et des Lettres" ernannt.

1974 Groucho erhält bei der Verleihung der Academy Awards den „Ehrenoscar für seine großartige Kreativität.

1977 Groucho, Harpo, Chico und Zeppo werden in die Ruhmeshalle Hollywoods aufgenommen. Gummo stirbt am 21. April. Groucho stirbt am 19. August.

30. November 1979 Zeppo stirbt.

1998 Das American Film Institute nimmt *Duck Soup (Die Marx Brothers im Krieg)* in die Liste der 100 größten amerikanischen Filme aller Zeiten auf.

CHRONOLOGIE

22 mars 1887 Marx naît à New York de parents juifs immigrés, Simon (Sam, dit aussi « Frenchie ») et Miene (Minnie).

23 novembre 1888 Naissance d'Adolph (Harpo) Marx.

2 octobre 1890 Naissance de Julius (Groucho) Marx.

23 octobre 1892 Naissance de Milton (Gummo) Marx.

25 février 1901 Naissance de Herbert (Zeppo) Marx.

1907 Groucho et Gummo font des tournées dans des spectacles de music-hall, rejoints par Harpo (1908) et Chico (1912). Zeppo remplace Gummo en 1918.

1920 Les frères Marx font leurs débuts au cinéma dans *Humorisk*, court-métrage muet perdu.

1924 *I'll Say She Is*, revue comique montée à Broadway, est saluée par Alexander Woollcott, critique dramatique très influent.

1925–1927 Succès de la comédie musicale *The Cocoanuts*, suivie par la production pour la scène d'Animal Crackers (1928).

1929 *Noix de coco*, premier long-métrage.

1931 S'installent à Hollywood pour tourner *Monnaie de singe*.

1932 Font la couverture du magazine *Time* comme phénomènes comiques.

1933 Échec commercial de *Soupe au canard*.

1934 Lassé de jouer les faire-valoir, Zeppo quitte la troupe des Marx.

1935 Premier film MGM des Marx produit par Irving Thalberg, *Une nuit à l'opéra* remporte un très grand succès critique et commercial. Avant le tournage, les blagues sont rôdées lors d'une tournée.

1936 Salvador Dalí leur écrit un scénario (jamais tourné) et envoie à Harpo une harpe aux cordes en fil de fer barbelé.

1947 Groucho anime un jeu radiophonique, « You Bet Your Life », adapté ensuite pour la télévision (1950-1961).

1949 *La Pêche au trésor*, dernier film du trio.

1959 Font leur dernière apparition en trio à la télévision dans « The Incredible Jewel Robbery », épisode du *General Electric Theater*. Groucho publie son autobiographie, *Mémoires capitales*, suivie des *Mémoires d'un amant lamentable* (1963) et de *Correspondance de Groucho Marx* (1967).

1961 Harpo publie son autobiographie, *Harpo et moi*. Chico meurt le 11 octobre.

28 septembre 1964 Mort de Harpo.

1972 Au festival de Cannes, Groucho est fait commandeur dans l'Ordre des Arts et des Lettres par le gouvernement français.

1974 Groucho reçoit un oscar à titre honorifique en reconnaissance de sa créativité brillante.

1977 Groucho, Harpo, Chico et Zeppo obtiennent chacun leur étoile dans le Hollywood Hall of Fame. Gummo meurt le 21 avril. Groucho meurt le 19 août.

30 November 1979 Mort de Zeppo.

1998 L'American Film Institute classe *Soupe au canard* parmi les cent plus grands films américains de tous les temps.

PORTRAIT FOR 'AT THE CIRCUS' (1939)
Harpo Marx

MARX BROTHERS MAKE NEW HIT

4

FILMOGRAPHY

FILMOGRAFIE

FILMOGRAPHIE

Humorisk (1920)
Harpo, Groucho, Chico.
Director/Regie/réalisation: Richard Smith.

Too Many Kisses (1925)
Harpo (The Village Peter Pan).
Director/Regie/réalisation: Paul Sloane.

A Kiss in the Dark (1925)
Zeppo (uncredited/ungenannt/non crédité).
Director/Regie/réalisation: Frank Tuttle.

The Cocoanuts (dt. *Cocoanuts*, fr. *Noix de coco*, 1929)
Groucho (Mr. Hammer), Harpo (Harpo), Chico (Chico), Zeppo (Jamison).
Director/Regie/réalisation: Robert Florey & Joseph Santley.

Animal Crackers (fr. *L'Explorateur en folie*, 1930)
Groucho (Captain/capitaine Jeffrey T. Spaulding), Harpo (The Professor/der Professor/le professeur), Chico (Signor Emanuel Ravelli), Zeppo (Horatio W. Jamison).
Director/Regie/réalisation: Victor Heerman.

Monkey Business (dt. *Die Marx Brothers auf See* [aka *Affentheater*], fr. *Monnaie de singe*, 1931)
Groucho, Harpo, Chico, Zeppo (as The Stowaways/als blinde Passagiere/les passagers clandestins), Sam 'Frenchie' Marx (Passenger on Ship and at Dock/Passagier auf dem Schiff und am Dock/un passager à bord et sur le quai).
Director/Regie/réalisation: Norman Z. McLeod.

The House That Shadows Built (1931)
Groucho (Caesar's Ghost/Cäsars Geist/le fantôme de César), Harpo (The Merchant of Wieners/Würstchenverkäufer/le marchand de saucisses), Chico (Tomalio), Zeppo (Sammy Brown).

Horse Feathers (dt. *Blühender Blödsinn*, fr. *Plumes de cheval*, 1932)
Groucho (Prof. Quincey Adams Wagstaff), Harpo (Pinky), Chico (Baravelli), Zeppo (Frank Wagstaff).
Director/Regie/réalisation: Norman Z. McLeod.

Hollywood on Parade No. 5 (1932)
Groucho, Harpo, Chico.
Director/Regie/réalisation: Louis Lewyn.

Duck Soup (dt. *Die Marx Brothers im Krieg*, fr. *Soupe de canard*, 1933)
Groucho (Rufus T. Firefly), Chico (Chicolini), Harpo (Pinkie), Zeppo (Bob Roland).
Director/Regie/réalisation: Leo McCarey.

Hollywood on Parade No. A-9 (1933)
Chico. Director/Regie/réalisation: Louis Lewyn.

Hollywood on Parade No. 11 (1933)
Groucho, Harpo. Director/Regie/réalisation: Louis Lewyn.

La Fiesta de Santa Barbara (1935)
Harpo. Director/Regie/réalisation: Louis Lewyn.

A Night at the Opera (*Die Marx Brothers in der Oper* [aka *Skandal in der Oper*], fr. *Une nuit à l'opéra*, 1935)
Groucho (Otis B. Driftwood), Chico (Fiorella), Harpo (Tomasso). Director/Regie/réalisation: Sam Wood.

Hollywood – The Second Step (1936)
Chico. Director/Regie/réalisation: Felix E. Feist.

A Day at the Races (dt. *Ein Tag beim Rennen* [aka *Das große Rennen/Auf der Rennbahn*], fr. *Un jour aux courses*, 1937)
Groucho (Dr. Hugh Z. Hackenbush), Chico (Tony), Harpo (Stuffy). Director/Regie/réalisation: Sam Wood.

Sunday Night at the Trocadero (1937)
Groucho. Director/Regie/réalisation: George Sidney.

Room Service (dt. *Zimmerdienst*, fr. *Panique à l'hôtel*, 1938)
Groucho (Gordon Miller), Chico (Harry Binelli), Harpo (Faker Englund). Director/Regie/réalisation: William A. Seiter.

At the Circus (dt. *Ein Tag im Zirkus* [aka *Die Marx Brothers im Zirkus*], fr. *Un jour au cirque*, 1939)
Groucho (Attorney/Rechtsanwalt/le procureur J. Cheever Loophole), Chico (Antonio), Harpo (Punchy). Director/Regie/réalisation: Edward Buzzell.

Go West (dt. *Die Marx Brothers im Wilden Westen*, fr. *Chercheurs d'or*, 1940)
Groucho (S. Quentin Quale), Chico (Joe Panello), Harpo ("Rusty" Panello).
Director/Regie/réalisation: Edward Buzzell.

The Big Store (dt. *Die Marx Brothers im Kaufhaus*, fr. *Les Marx au grand magasin*, 1941)

Groucho (Wolf J. Flywheel), Chico (Ravelli), Harpo (Wacky). Director/Regie/réalisation: Charles Reisner.

Screen Snapshots Series 23, No. 2 (1943)
Groucho. Director/Regie/réalisation: Ralph Staub.

Screen Snapshots Series 23, No. 8 (1943)
Groucho, Harpo, Chico. Director/Regie/réalisation: Ralph Staub.

Stage Door Canteen (1943)
Harpo. Director/Regie/réalisation: Frank Borzage.

The All-Star Bond Rally (1945)
Harpo. Director/Regie/réalisation: Michael Audley.

A Night in Casablanca (dt. *Eine Nacht in Casablanca*, fr. *Une nuit à Casablanca*, 1946)
Groucho (Ronald Kornblow), Harpo (Rusty), Chico (Corbaccio). Director/Regie/réalisation: Archie Mayo.

Copacabana (1947)
Groucho (Lionel Q. Devereaux). Director/Regie/réalisation: Alfred E. Green.

Love Happy (dt. *Die Marx Brothers im Theater* [aka *Glücklich verliebt*], fr. *La Pêche au trésor*, 1949)
Groucho (Detective/Privatdetektiv/le détective Sam Grunion), Harpo (Harpo), Chico (Faustino the Great/Faustino der Große/le grand Faustino). Director/Regie/réalisation: David Miller & Leo McCarey (uncredited/ungenannt/non crédités).

Mr. Music (1950)
Groucho. Director/Regie/réalisation: Richard Hadyn.

Double Dynamite (dt. *Doppeltes Dynamit*, 1951)
Groucho (Emil J. Keck). Director/Regie/réalisation: Irving Cummings.

A Girl in Every Port (dt. *In jedem Hafen eine Braut*, fr. *Une fille dans chaque port*, 1952)
Groucho (Benny Linn). Director/Regie/réalisation: Chester Erskine.

Will Success Spoil Rock Hunter? (dt. *Sirene in blond*, fr. *La Blonde explosive*, 1957)
Groucho (Georgie Schmidlapp).
Director/Regie/réalisation: Frank Tashlin.

The Story of Mankind (1957).
Groucho (Peter Minuit), Harpo (Isaac Newton), Chico (Monk). Director/Regie/réalisation: Irwin Allen.

Showdown at Ulcer Gulch (1958)
Groucho, Chico. Director/Regie/réalisation: Shamus Culhane.

Skidoo (dt. *Skidoo – Ein Happening in Love*, 1968)
Groucho ("God"/„Gott"/« Dieu »).
Director/Regie/réalisation: Otto Preminger.

"This is a genuine beaver. . . the last of its kind. The beavers have stopped making them!"

BIBLIOGRAPHY

Adamson, Joe: *Groucho, Harpo, Chico and Sometimes Zeppo: A Celebration of the Marx Brothers*. Pocket Books, 1973.
Allen, Miriam Marx (ed.): *Love, Groucho: Letters from Groucho Marx to His Daughter Miriam*. Da Capo Press, 2002.
Anobile, Richard J.: *Why a Duck? Visual and Verbal Gems from the Marx Brothers Movies*. Darien House, 1971.
Arce, Hector: *Groucho*. Putnam, 1979.
Bego, Mark: *The Marx Brothers*. Pocket Essentials, 2001.
Benayoun, Robert: *Les Marx Brothers ont la parole*. Seuil, 1991.
Bergan, Ronald: *The Life and Times of the Marx Brothers*. Popular Culture Ink, 1992.
Crichton, Kyle Samuel: *The Marx Brothers*. Doubleday, 1950.
Eyles, Allen: *The Complete Films of the Marx Brothers*. Citadel Press, 1992.
Gehring, Wes D.: *The Marx Brothers: A Bio-Bibliography*. Greenwood, 1987.
Hobsch, Manfred: *Film ab: Die Marx Brothers*. Schwarzkopf & Schwarzkopf, 2001.
Hoppe, Ulrich: *Die Marx Brothers: Ihre Filme, ihr Leben*. Heyne, 1985.
Kanfer, Stefan: *Groucho: The Life and Times of Julius Henry Marx*. Knopf, 2000.
Lightfoot, Roger (ed.): *The Marx Brothers Poster Book*. Zachary Kwintner Books, 1991.
Louvish, Simon: *Monkey Business: The Lives and Legends of the Marx Brothers*. Thomas Dunne Books, 2000.
Marx, Arthur: *My Life with Groucho: Growing Up with the Marx Brothers*. Barricade Books, 1992.
Marx Brothers: *Les Marx brothers: Pensées, répliques et anecdotes*. Le Cherche-Midi, 1995.
Marx, Groucho: *Groucho and Me*. Da Capo Press, 1995.
Marx, Groucho: *The Groucho Letters: Letters from and to Groucho Marx*. Da Capo Press, 1994.
Marx, Groucho & Anobile, Richard J.: *The Marx Brothers Scrapbook*. HarperCollins, 1989.
Marx, Groucho & Bader, Robert (ed.): *Groucho Marx and Other Short Stories and Tall Tales*. Faber & Faber, 1996.
Marx, Harpo & Barber, Rowland: *Harpo Speaks!* Limelight Editions, 2004.
Marx, Maxine: *Growing Up with Chico*. Limelight Editions, 1986.
Mitchell, Glenn: *The Marx Brothers Encyclopedia*. Reynolds & Hearn, 2003.
Nolden, Rainer: *Die Marx Brothers*. Rowohlt Tb., 2002.
Seaton, George et al.: *The Marx Brothers: Monkey Business, Duck Soup and A Day at the Races*. Faber & Faber, 1993.
Tchernoff, Alexis: *Les Marx Brothers*. Pygmalion, 1997.

Video Documentaries
Inside the Marx Brothers. KOCH Entertainment Distribution, 2003.
The Marx Brothers in a Nutshell. Whyaduck Productions, 2004.
The Unknown Marx Brothers. Wellspring, 1993.

Websites
www.imdb.com
www.marx-brothers.org/
www.whyaduck.com/index.htm

IMPRINT

Hohenzollernring 53, D-50672 Köln
www.taschen.com

Editor/Picture Research/Layout: Paul Duncan/Wordsmith Solutions
Editorial Coordination: Martin Holz, Cologne
Production Coordination: Nadia Najm and Horst Neuzner, Cologne
German Translation: Thomas J. Kinne, Nauheim
French Translation: Jean-François Cornu, Nantes
Multilingual Production: www.arnaudbriand.com, Paris
Typeface Design: Sense/Net, Andy Disl and Birgit Reber, Cologne

Printed in Italy
ISBN 978-3-8228-2219-7

To stay informed about upcoming TASCHEN titles, please request our magazine at www.taschen.com/magazine or write to TASCHEN, Hohenzollernring 53, D-50672 Cologne, Germany, contact@taschen.com, fax: +49-221-254919. We will be happy to send you a free copy of our magazine which is filled with information about all of our books.

All the photos in this book, except for those listed below, were supplied by The Kobal Collection.
The Jim Heimann Collection: pp. 46/47, 98/99, 101, 112, 186.
British Film Institute Stills, Posters and Designs, London: pp. 6/7, 18, 22, 24, 25, 28, 29, 34/35, 38, 39, 52, 53, 62/63, 72, 73, 78, 79, 80, 81, 91, 94/95, 96, 100, 108, 109, 118, 119, 121, 122, 124, 133, 134, 135, 136/137, 138, 139, 145, 151, 154, 156/157, 158, 163, 165, 168, 176/177, 178.
Thanks to Dave Kent, Phil Moad and everybody at The Kobal Collection for their professionalism and kindness.